T0365765

Dreaming New Schools

Inspiring Lifelong Learning through Conscious Creativity

Angela Benedetto, PhD

Balboa Press books may be ordered through booksellers or by contacting:

Balboa Press
A Division of Hay House
1663 Liberty Drive
Bloomington, IN 47403
www.balboapress.com
844-682-1282

Interior Graphics/Art Credit - Jessica Nock & Paul Hoffman

ISBN: 978-1-4525-7323-6 (sc)
ISBN: 978-1-4525-7322-9 (e)

Library of Congress Control Number: 2013907687

Print information available on the last page.

Balboa Press rev. date: 03/07/2025

In Gratitude,

I dedicate this text to the countless teens whose creativity and intelligence has gone unnoticed or been unsupported.

Thanks to my parents, Michael, and Nancy Benedetto. You are forever in my loving memory.

Heartfelt thanks to the late Elinor O'Hare, whose generosity, made the publishing of this project possible.

I express gratitude to my ancestors, who provided a strong lineage imbued with loyalty, devotion, dedication and *"groundedness"*.

I send thanks across the universe to the late Maya Author, Marcia Dale Lopez, and to Brooks Barton-Green. Their wisdom, devotion and unwavering love are qualities I hope to imbue. Their generosity of spirit and contribution to this body of work are appreciated in countless ways.

Special thanks to Shelly Hagen, for your editorial assistance.

Thanks to my daughter and son, Jessica, and Matthew for your book cover design and book layout.

Exceptional thanks to Paul Hoffman for his "fine tooth approach" in cover, editing and image design.

Thank you, Rosanne Ranari, and Joe Bruchac. Your support in the film, Dreaming New Schools inspired me to complete this book.

A warm thank you goes to the many students I have had the privilege to serve in the New York State public school system. They taught me the value of being a life-long learner, and what an amazing ride we've had!

Lastly, I thank my adult children, Jessica, Jonathan, and Matthew. I have learned in countless ways through the marvelous life we shared, in beauty and challenge, in devotion and joy, mystery, and wonder. May we continue to grow in love's embrace.

A note from the author: It's been nearly a decade since I wrote Dreaming New Schools, and I still have much to learn in the school some call life. As I revisited the original text, I sensed an undercurrent of my own unresolved frustration from working in a large inner-city school system, reflected in some of the sections of the text. My intention was and still is, to share some of my discoveries as teacher and student. In the spirit of practicing life-long learning, I invite you to explore many facets of learning offered, and their potential for transformation. Many blessing to the generations who follow.

Throughout time symbols have been used to convey meaning. The symbols used on the book's cover and in the text relate to the content in each chapter. Symbols can have different meanings in many cultures. The descriptions below describe the significance of the symbols used in *Dreaming New Schools* as they apply to each chapter.

Fire Yantra : Energy, Action

Yin Yang: Balance , Intuitive & Intellect

Nature: Balance Between Elements

Love, Compassion,
Openness, Collaboration

Water, Ether: Fluidity, Energy Body

PI: Math, Logic, Reason

Music, Harmonics, Vibration

Ohm, Universal Sound,
Creation, Eastern Philosophy

Wisdom, Action

Caduceus: Alchemy, Healing

Infinity: Unlimited

Contents

Literacy of the Heart
Written by Angela
May 2009

How can we have a positive, sustaining influence on our children individually and collectively? What are the experiences our children encounter to learn about themselves and the communities where they live? And how can we best help them to process, vocalize, and fully understand those experiences?

Two traumatic events compelled me to ask these questions.

On April 2, 2009, students and staff at Schenectady High School were informed of another suicide. This was the fourth African American student to take her life, during the 2008-2009 school year, adding to the school's grim total of eight suicides in in less than four years. The devastating news plunged our high school into despair and uncertainty.

Together, through steadfast dedication- SHS students, staff, and community leaders quickly responded through positive action.

I take this time to honor all those impacted by our heartbreaking loss and extend warm thoughts of hope and healing.

The second event, which pales in light of the aforementioned tragedy directly impacted my students, which is why I'm sharing it here. One week after the suicide, students and I were shocked by an article posted in the local news stating that our Family & Consumer Science Program was to be cut the following year.

Students in my "Children in Crisis" class had spent the prior week sharing, and fine tuning their intervention term projects. They were concerned about completing their graduation requirements and what school would be like without FACS courses that focused on topics relevant to their lives.

One student made a comment that the district should cut the Foods & Nutrition portion of the FACS program because, she felt it wasn't as important as other courses on the chopping block. A student named Fatima disagreed, "This decision-making process gets complicated", she explained. "How can we determine what is of more value to someone else"? The students listened carefully. It was obvious in that moment that they clearly understood the value of respecting differing viewpoints. And from there, the students saw themselves as agents of change.

Fatima stepped into her role as "student-leader," organizing a petition with over fifteen hundred signatures, and attending the board meeting. Other students followed, sharing their viewpoints at those meetings. I saw this as nothing less than remarkable.

Fatima was born in Sudan and arrived in the U.S. at the age of 12. Now a senior, she demonstrated what she had learned in just four short years – intellectual, emotional, and social growth – with grace, compassion and foresight. Fatima saw beyond her needs and advocated for the next generation of high school students at the end of her high school career! These actions hit the very core of what schools can teach children: Think globally, solve problems, and care for others. I call this Literacy of the Heart.

On the most basic level, students need to feel safe and well cared for to grow and flourish – personally, socially, physically and intellectually. We know that many children struggle with self-care, self-love and feeling empowered.

Even as I share our story, I am aware that I am one instructor, working in one small community, connected to the larger global learning community, on our precious planet. Our story is a small part of that greater whole, with many opportunities to transform disparity into hope.

Human dignity, equality, and self-awareness become the cornerstones on which deeper levels of self-actualization can flourish. I truly believe that these skills are attainable, but the structure of our present school systems must become flexible enough to facilitate these changes. Through my years of teaching, I have learned that children who are raised in violence and extreme poverty must physically see the value of sustaining hope and making change through learning if they are going to demonstrate those values in their own lives. I witnessed this first-hand as students demonstrated creativity and compassion in in their choice to attend meetings, organize fund-raisers, and develop intervention projects to share with their peers. It is my sincere hope that school administrators and teaching staff strive to create harmony, inclusion, and unity in their learning communities.

We need not wait for crisis to choose a peaceful path of resolution. As we gain confidence in our inner- wisdom, we model those attributes to the students in our care through our actions.

And actions DO speak louder than words.

"I've got a dream, that one day…"
Dr. Martin Luther King Jr.

1 SHS students and advisors from several clubs, volunteer as part of the Suicide Intervention healing initiative, Spring 2010

Introduction

When I first wrote Dreaming New Schools, I was eager to share everything I'd learned through my doctoral studies, hoping to support others who feel called to work with students. You can find the film Dreaming New Schools, on YouTube. I hope you enjoy the interviews from students, teachers, artists, and scholars who share their ideas about creativity and learning.

Learning is a creative process. Since the earliest recorded time, human beings have learned through discovery and direct experience. Through creativity, students are given the possibility to dream, and it is in the dreaming they find hope in hopeless circumstances. Students are seeking creative ways to demonstrate their intelligence in a system is only beginning to explore the value of cultivating self-reflective, resilient skills in youth and adults who work with youth. Balance between intellect and intuition (or conscious creativity) is *necessary* to develop wholesome, stable, creative skills that facilitate discovering our inner genius. When creative approaches to learning are denied, these vital skills become atrophied over time.

How do we design "learning communities" that grow our human potential?

The human mind and body are like gold mines; and our capacity for growth is a continuum of limitless possibility. We are creators by nature, continually developing consciously and unconsciously. Growth into transformation is a natural process when met with dignity, respect, and great reverence.

There is no other institution with the equal opportunity to shape young minds and support students in reaching their potential. Shifting our orientation to consider learning as an interconnected system can have amazing results.

As students and teachers identify and understand the multiple intelligences available to them, they have the opportunity to explore their unique style of learning. Modeling multiple intelligences helps students and adults appreciate individually unique expressions of these intelligences.

In this practice, we experience a deeper understanding of interrelatedness and connectivity in the learning community. Today's schools can prepare to enter the level of advancement that would nurture the innate creativity of each child and inspire them to reach their potential. We can take our cues from the advances in technology, medicine, science, psychology, and consciousness studies– all within the last decade alone. Intuitive, process-oriented skills offer great potential for teachers and students.

Education in its most authentic sense has the unique opportunity to be at the forefront of creative change, social justice, growth, and transformation. Students are seeking opportunities to think and live more authentically. The potential is available for authentic educational reform that empowers both the teacher and student. If change can happen in one classroom, then it's quite possible for an entire building, and even a school system to grow beyond the current structure. I believe we can create inclusive learning networks that enhance our creativity, expand our hearts, and bring joy and satisfaction for all.

Benefit the Child, Benefit the Community

Creating learning environments suitable for all children requires focused attention to the needs of the community, finances, and resources to back this action. Our local and Federal government, alongside agencies vested in the future of **all children** can support school administrators who are willing to live this process. as leaders of the school community, they can model inclusion and cooperative decision-making into school policies, curriculum, format, and budgets.

Learning is an individual process when we consider individual perceptual skills. It is impossible to create a standardized test that will honor and demonstrate our multiple intelligences. This is why I encourage educational leaders on all levels to creatively explore what learning means to them personally and remember their passion for teaching and being lifelong learners. Personal reflection can have an amazing impact on discovering ways that children can be guided to explore and experience their unique potential.

At-risk youth require special attention. Many are disconnected from family, and community. CONNECTION IS A BASIC HUMAN NEED INTRINSIC TO US ALL. Here's where relational learning, connecting with, and discovering the uniquely creative qualities of each student *must* work hand-in-hand with academic studies. Relational learning holds a reverence for the sanctity of human life and acknowledges that each person we encounter is of equal value and worth. Self-discovery can take shape through a variety of forms. How we approach the content is what's most important.

When children are encouraged to explore the deeper aspects of themselves and expand their unique talents and gifts, learning becomes an inter-personal experience that they can relate to. Competition takes a back seat as each student is encouraged to experience his or herself as uniquely creative. Standards become a personal benchmark rather than a competitive experience with classmates. Students develop self-esteem as they are honored for being uniquely creative beings. And because relational school experiences build confidence, communities benefit as youngsters grow and learn to appreciate our sameness and differences, they can feel safe enough to meet the challenges of adulthood.

I believe teaching is sacred work. An educator's presence in the classroom has a powerful impact on the students they engage with. This impact goes *far* beyond the delivery of a lecture or assistance with class work. Teaching and learning are partners in our future. A harmonious stimulating environment invites a graceful exchange of ideas where student and teacher feel safe to explore learning.

Creative solutions thrive in this environment. The world changes for the better.

Empowering the Public

I invite you into a provocative public discussion concerning how public education is presented in the 21st century, and ask the following questions:

What values, skills, and learning methods are we imparting to our future generations? Can we create opportunities for learning that are inclusive, life-affirming, creative, challenging, and globally aware. Imagine the benefits!

Many educators are at a loss for dreaming of change, but I believe that schools can be designed to support the adults who have taken students under their wing. There is an urgent call to remember the power of dreaming without limitation, and the transformative power of self-love, and putting those dreams into action. We have the possibility to transform this world if, we choose, through our actions, words, and deeds. We *can* make a difference! And schools are the perfect environment to have a radical impact on our future generations.

It takes courage and effort to speak up when something is not working. And remaining silent, takes an immense toll on the mind and spirit, to say nothing of those being directly affected. We can make an honest evaluation of the present-day school system without judgment and place our focus on what is most needed at this auspicious time in history! This text is a call for social action of the bravest kind, from within our own hearts and minds.

Are we willing to become scientists of the most authentic ranking, discovering our own self-sourced power, intelligence, wisdom, harmony, and joy? What a blast this could be!!!! Schools can provide the opportunity for children and young adults to explore their passions, grow their talents, develop their aptitudes and skills, and become lifelong learners – *regardless of the age.*

Inner Vision

We've forgotten how to dream.
We didn't mean to.
It just happened.
Somewhere …
Between childhood and adulthood
In the time we spend trying to figure things out,
Or do things correctly,
Or be more mature,
Or be more responsible,
Or trying to fit in,
Or grow up.
We've forgotten how to dream,
And in our forgetting,
We've forgotten to honor our children's dreams.
We want them to "grow up."
To "get big" to "get serious" to "get real",
And we've forgotten the power of the dream,
For in the dream lies the seed to our inner passion and our wild imaginings.
And through dreaming we are all connected,
For we are free to explore, free to realize,
to create, to invent, and to explore once more.
In the dream we are free to give and receive love.
We've forgotten how to dream, but only for a moment in time.
In the twinkling of a star, we return to our dream.
In the glistening morning dewdrop, we return,
Empty yet full, open to receive.

In the pause between each breath, we feel our heartbeat.
Calling us deep within to experience
this precious moment, dreaming once more.
-- from Angela's journal 2005

2 dreamstime

Chapter One

"Courage is an inner resolution to go forward despite obstacles."
Dr. Martin Luther King Jr.

The Five Principles of Transformative Learning

The five principles of transformative learning are discoveries I made during my internship as a Ph.D. candidate. The principles offer a framework for the experience of learning as transformation. They include:

(1) We are Multidimensional Beings
(2) We have the Potential to Access Wisdom on Many Creative Levels
(3) Using Intellect and Intuition Creates Balance
(4) Learning Holistically Supports Growth and Transformation
(5) Small Learning Communities Support Transformative Learning

The early stages of these principles developed through observations I made during my clinical experience with sound healing practitioners and energy healers using the laws of harmonics. They evolved into a set of principles as the research project took shape. Unlike cognitive skills, sensory learning is holistic; that is, sensory learning includes the body in the learning process. Sound, rhythm, and music are sensory experiences that engage the body.

Within this framework, I view the role of the educator as one who guides the learner in the unfolding of his or her potential in terms of conscious evolution, personally, socially, intellectually, and beyond. I see learning as a continual process offering opportunity for expansion, depth, understanding and development for both learner and educator.

Schools have taken great care in developing programs designed to develop cognitive skills. We give students lots of information to memorize, read, analyze, and ultimately conceptualize. Cognitive learning can be greatly enhanced through increased perceptual experiences.

As we grow older, we realize that learning in its truest sense occurs through the experiences we've had, not the information we've gathered. We use information to expand our thoughts and ideas, and that's great. Sensory learning recognizes our body's innate intelligence. Practicing mindfulness helps us experience and explore our consciousness.

Indigenous peoples across cultures share an understanding that the mysteries of the cosmos are literally stored in the cells of our body. Our bodies are the vehicles for our Spirit. Our quest for discovery has been supported by science for centuries. Self-discovery has been left for the individual to master independent of family, education, and scientific models until recent time. Self-discovery opens the doorway towards self-acceptance and wholeness. Schools that encourage self-discovery expand creativity.

We experience glimpses of our unity, harmony, joy, and peace -- watching a sunset, hearing the first songbird in springtime, or holding a newborn baby. We recognize the sanctity of life and creation itself. Through witnessing, sensing, being with nature, we remember that we are co-creators in our own world. Where we choose to place our focus will have a tremendous impact on our life experiences. It's important to encourage self-discovery as early as possible.

Educators can offer opportunities for learners to explore through introspection, and experimentation. Learners have the opportunity to change their orientation, their outlook and, ultimately, their behavior through transformation. Educators can be coached to use interdisciplinary and integrative approaches in the classroom. Experiential learning offers the opportunity for the body and mind to function as a unified whole.

On a basic level, the educator's role is to inspire the learner while challenging him or her to explore and reach his or her potential. It is important to honor different learning styles and offer opportunities for students to fully engage in the learning process while encouraging self-awareness. Students can explore why it is both meaningful and important to increase their knowledge of a given field of study, mastering the content they are engaged in. They also discover the interconnection of a given area of study and its *impact on others*.

Introducing Mindfulness

Watch a child learning through play, and see if you can find the magic, they experience in learning something new. Being the head teacher of the Early Childhood Program at Schenectady High School offered many opportunities to observe children of all ages and their developmental stages and learning techniques. Angie discovered how important it was to honor my student's learning styles.

Many researchers in education and educational psychology agree that we express and demonstrate our intelligence various ways.

Pioneers in the field of mindfulness and emotional intelligence, have expanded their research to public schools, offering students opportunities for personal growth that go beyond the educational standards. Programs including Jon Kabat Zinn's *MBSR*, Linda Lantieri's *Inner Resilience* program, Goldie Hawn's *Mind Up* curriculum, and other research-based collaborative models support self- awareness and personal growth.

I noticed the profoundly positive effects of using relaxation techniques and mindfulness exercises in my classroom. It was years later that I learned that there was hard science supporting what I sensed intuitively. The increased levels of cortisol to the pre-frontal cortex, helps increase attention, and increased levels of serotonin, improves the social/ emotional state of being through the practice of mindfulness. Jon Kabat Zinn, Ph.D. began is research in mindfulness and its impact on stress, emotional hardiness in 1982 at the University of Massachusetts Center for Mindfulness in Health Care, Medicine, and Society. Since 1982, continued research in MBSR has been conducted by scientists in psychology and neuroscience in many universities including clinical trials at the University of Wisconsin, UCLA, the University of Whales and Cambridge, UK. This long-standing research demonstrates that mindfulness practiced over time increases in grey matter density, helping them act "effectively under stress". You can visit the MBSR

Linda Lantieri's powerful work was seen as a necessary program to help children cultivate resilience and emotional intelligence after the twin towers were bombed on 9/11. Several New York City schools were within the parameters of ground zero when the planes hit the Twin Towers. The devastating impact of this crisis became the enormous catalyst for a much-needed change in the way schooling and learning is presented in public education.

Gardner is keenly aware of the importance of a continuing dialog on this topic. He recognized that world spiritual leaders, such as Gandhi, Mandela, and Martin Luther King Jr. have (or have had) qualities that would depict them as being more spiritually aware than the average person (Gardner 89). Gardner describes his own relationship to music as one, which approximates a spiritual experience (93).

website for more juicy research. Gina Biegel's Stress Reduction Workbook for Teens is a wonderful teaching tool.

Research-based curriculum supporting inner resilience and emotional intelligence is becoming increasingly more accessible. The Hawn Foundation "mind-up" mindfulness curriculum has been implemented in over one thousand schools in Canada and the US. The University of Mass. has been doing pioneering research in Mindfulness and stress reduction. The implications for cultivating self- awareness, resilience, and mindfulness as a normal part of school curriculum can help all those involved in schools stay more focused, maintain balance throughout the day, and tap into their innate intelligence.

Howard Gardner's model of Multiple Intelligence gives a foundation for academic institutions to educate students by acknowledging that there are multiple ways in which we may demonstrate our intelligence (Gardner). In his most recent text, ***Intelligence Reframed***, Gardner discusses that although he has added two new intelligences to his model -- natural and existential intelligence. While Gardner states that he has not personally experienced existential intelligence, he repeatedly uses the word "spiritual" in his discourse on existential intelligence. His support of existential intelligence implies that models, which explore the experience of existence, (such as existential or) are, indeed, relevant to learning styles. Scientists and scholars who are comfortable with spirituality within the context of their research, such as Einstein, Maslow, Jung, Beaulieu, Berendt, Arrien, and Broomfield, may not have difficulty including Gardner's eighth and ninth intelligences.

Looking Forward

The onset of the age of technology has brought remarkable changes in gathering, compiling, and analyzing information. Communication has never been easier to accomplish in terms of speed and accuracy. We can take creative responsibility for our actions. We cannot change the past, but we can consciously and honestly assess our present state and have a positive impact on our future. Our children, our planet, and beyond depend on this. Evolution is an ongoing process, which we have a grand opportunity to actively participate in!

Chapter Two

"Let life get wind of you."
Tama J. Keives

Principle One: We are Multi-Dimensional Creative Beings

Mind-Body Integration

Experiencing ourselves as Multi-Dimensional Creative Beings opens the door for infinite possibility. Including the body in the learning process is central to holistic learning and personal transformation. Somatic Theory (Somatics) is one model demonstrating body-mind integration. Somatics explores our creative nature, or essence, as in *all* aspects of the body. The body is understood to be intelligent down to the cellular level, and the mind is not seen as being the most important aspect of the body, nor is any other part of the body.

Years before I began my Ph.D., I took a weeklong training at Naropa Institute with cellular Biologist Bruce Lipton, Ph. D. and leader in Somatic Psychology, Susan Apoyshan. In her work ***Natural Intelligence***, Susan Aposhyan describes the body's intelligence as an intrinsic part of learning, "As long as we are merely aware of a part of ourselves, it (the body) is not empowered to fully participate" (Aposhyan 11). "Each of our basic tissue and fluid types have their own unique qualities and creative resources, on a cellular level we have a basic intelligence that is universal" (Apoyshan 11). Including our body in the learning experience can have a profound impact on our learning experience.

Lipton agrees with Aposhyan. In his book, *The Biology of Belief*, Lipton researched how our perceptions affect the very makeup of our cellular structure. Lipton maintains that our cells are intelligent, that they are not genetically controlled, and the harmful perceptions created through negative thoughts, which cause damage to our cellular structure, can be relearned. According to Lipton, the biological makeup of cells can physically change the process of introducing affirming thoughts. This theory supports the body's intelligence as a unified whole. Being aware of the body's systems plays an important role in healing the body and mind, expanding our innate intelligence.

Connecting with the Energy Body

Somatics cultivates awareness with the body as a long-term and multifaceted practice. This practice is subtle, yet very important because it invites the creativity of our body's expanded resources (Aposhyan 11). Somatic Theory is based on four principles:

(1) Body-mind reintegration is a respectful response. The body is approached with respect of its intelligence.
(2) This respect is demonstrated through full participation striving to be aware with the body.
(3) Inclusiveness with all aspects of the body and mind must be consciously included.
(4) Integration requires dialogue. (Apoyshan, Naropa Institute)

The principles of Somatics lay the groundwork for a deep understanding of inclusion and integrative learning individually and collectively.

I didn't fully understand Somatic Theory until I began working with energy healers during my Ph.D. internship. In 2013, I explored human consciousness with Brooks in Manhattan. Brooks had a profound capacity to hold sacred space with keen depth and perception. He held a crystal-clear energetic field in full awareness of the participants, me included, which expanded our capacity to experience our unique multi-dimensional perception. I felt my body's energy expand and fill the room; Graceful, and vast in the simplicity of complete harmony as it permeated in and beyond my body, and my Being. I keenly sensed the very life force that animated Manhattan as we walked to lunch in a nearby restaurant after our morning session. I could actually see the energy of creation in everything I witnessed. The colors of the trees, the buildings, and the busy hustle and bustle of Seventy Second Street were more vibrant than I'd ever experienced.

The depth of this level of knowing is difficult to describe, but still resides in me. Sensing myself from this expanded state has taught me that I am indeed a multi-dimensional being, whose perceptual abilities continue to evolve.

I'm not always in harmony, but having experienced the non-physical part of me, makes it easier for me to take a step back and notice when I am out of balance, perceiving experiences from a less expanded view.

I now understand that moment to moment, I can choose to expand my perception. I feel more at ease opening to my vulnerabilities and am less likely to avoid or deny them. As I open my heart, I gain wisdom. This is Somatics in its purist form, exploring who I am as my body, without conditioning from family, society, or life experiences.

Adolescents are changing and growing so rapidly that it is only logical that they are incredibly preoccupied with their bodies. Primary and secondary teachers and students can benefit from courses that promote body-mind awareness like Somatic studies. These principles ask the participant to look beyond the cultural belief that there is inherent conflict between individual bodily impulses and social order. In other words, Somatics demonstrates that by being engaged in our bodies at the sensate level, we can feel the sensations that arise from internal events and our response to those events, as well as the integration of our internal and external sensations. We can then express a unified response, which balances our inner and outer needs without conflict.

Participation with nature, movement, music, the arts, and experiential learning engage the body and mind, providing the opportunity for growth and change. It might feel strange, or even frightening, but I invite educators to creatively explore with their students. Take students out of the classroom when you can. Meeting with teachers who are willing to collaborate and do something creative and TALKING about your experiences will contribute to transforming the school culture. Having discussions with your students creates a sense of stability and authenticity and a connection that is unbreakable. Teachers can cultivate opportunities for sensitive learners to use their intuitive skills – in other words, to integrate the *whole* person– to promote balance, health, and positive change.

In many traditions, *teachers,* and *healers* (both the words and the people) are one in the same. This can be the case in our culture as well, and there is no better subject for teachers to lead students in than connecting with the energy body. Why is this, you may ask? Our energy bodies and emotional bodies are constantly interacting with one another. As a result, we empathetically sense the feelings of those near us and mistake them for our own! Our energy body also interacts with our physical body, resulting in energy flow or energy blockages in our physical. But when our body's energy flows uninterrupted, we experience health, well-being, and emotional balance. These qualities certainly accelerate the learning process.

Indigenous cultures, mystics and leaders in the human potential movement acknowledge the presence of our energy through different terminology, such as *light* or *luminescence.* I discovered through my internship in the *light energy body* and other contemplative practices such as yoga and meditation that an individual can intuitively develop skill in balancing their energy through practice.

This is far from a new concept. There is an understanding within Eastern practices and teachings that we are multi-dimensional, multi-sensory beings, and spiritual teachers, healers and shamans access information from many dimensions or states of consciousness. Grof describes the merging of ancient wisdom teachings and contemporary scientific inquiry as in "the outermost reaches of human consciousness research, we discover that science has taken us full circle to a vision of our lives as being very much like that described by the wise elders of ancient and Oriental cultures" (Grof 90).

Spirit is the *"stuff"* that we are made of. It's not really about religion, although its origins seem exist in most religious texts. For centuries, mystics and shamans across cultures bypassed the organization they may have been born into seeking direct contact with their spiritual nature, and the cosmos, developing the ability to bypass the natural order of what we've been taught as being nature. I've experienced my mind literally expanding in consciousness, like waves of energy, and sparkling effervescence, I've walked on hot coals, without a trace of heat, and heard my brother Mike's voice shortly after he passed. Indigenous Ecuadorian Elder, Anton Ponce DeLeon shared how his grandfather, the elder of the Quichuan community's tent become filled with light as his body literally disappeared into the ethers, in his passing. Marcia Dale Lopez communicated with several members of her beloved community after passing. If Spirit is recognized as the animating life force from which we originate, then the evolution of our consciousness plays an important role in our lifecycles and history as human beings. Science is corroborating with the understanding of a unified energetic field from which all creation has individuated. I am not an expert in this field, but I am curious about the many experiences I have encountered that indicate that everything is energy, and energy (and consciousness) exists in several dimensions simultaneously. Could it be that our body expressed as energy is not limited to a religious experience based on beliefs, but a conscious experience?

Energy healers who have highly developed visual skills may actually be able to see or sense the field of energy, which surrounds the body. *During a session with South American Shaman Don Jose Pinedas in 2001, I could sense the expansion of my auric energy field (which surrounds the body) projecting at least six feet from my body. My energy felt very smooth and light, almost tactile. When I got on the subway to return home, it felt as if I was in a cocoon of energy, whose borders lightly pressed against the subway walls. I felt this in waves, circulating around and through my body, bringing balance and peace.*

In 2004, I had three sessions with the late Dr. Marcia Dale Lopez, Ph.D. Marcia worked intuitively with the energy body for over two decades. I discovered that through conscious choice, I could uncover limiting belief patterns, sense these patterns, and remove them from my energy field. The sessions gave me a sense of freedom with an entirely new perspective resulting from the clarity that I gained. It's been nearly a decade since I've written this book, and since that time, I've had many encounters walking between two worlds, the physical, and non-physical. sensing, hearing, or seeing beyond what Shaman's call "ordinary reality". I've received messages from the other side and seen family members who have crossed. I met a benevolent clan of Sasquatch in real time a Jaguar Spirit in Amazonia, and baby Jesus in dream time. I've been healed by a group of dolphins in Hawaii, whose sonar sent waves of unconditional love through my being, for hours. I experienced my mind expanding into unity consciousness for a brief moment. I've heard messages from tree beings, and beings that live inside the earth. (Although it's taken a decade for me to feel fully comfortable sharing this new information here), these encounters have redefined my experience as a multi-dimensional being, expressing my most authentic self, inspiring hope for humanity's future.

Experiences that were originally framed as research, which became a part of my daily life are difficult to measure by current scientific standards and are best described by the individual directly involved. The late Transpersonal Psychologist, Marcia Dale Lopez, Ph.D. describes standardization as an "insult" explaining that mechanical tests are not an accurate assessment of 'who we are' (as Multi-Dimensional Creative Beings), because "Who we are is constantly changing." Learning is an evolutionary process. I invite educators to take the evolutionary leap forward, supporting each child's potential by honoring and respecting their learning styles and orientation. In doing so, you can create healing out of teaching.

Physical Boundaries — Real or Imagined?

Research in human consciousness of the past few years has begun to show us that our physical boundaries may be much more illusionary than real. The onset of alternative therapies, which use energy systems in or surrounding the body, demonstrate a growing interest in the field of energy medicine, particularly in the United States, where there is an increasing presence of holistic alternative therapies integration including chiropractic, homeopathy, reflexology, shiatsu, acupressure, acupuncture, ayurveda, reiki, kinesiology, massage therapy, qigong, and therapeutic touch.

Many people swear by acupuncture to rid the body of everything from allergies to the desire to smoke cigarettes. Acupuncture is derived from classical Chinese medicine, which in turn is rooted in ancient Chinese cosmology. "The Chinese believed that the vital force or *ch'i* circulates in the body through meridians, traveling a set route between organs and systems" (Willis 118). If you've ever gone to an acupuncturist or chiropractor who is well versed in subtle energy flow and gentle touch, you may have experienced the flow of energy in your body, and their expansion through treatments which open the energy meridians, or channels.

How does this relate to education? Acupuncture (along with other Eastern healing practices) has become so commonplace, it's difficult to imagine that only 50 years ago, it was considered very strange and was not covered by Western insurance companies. As increasingly more patients receive relief and healing from alternative therapies, it has gained credence and acceptance in the Western world. The changes I am suggesting to our current education system may seem alien right now, but many are based on the Eastern influences of seeing the student as an energetic being. How long will it be until these ideas receive the same type of acceptance as holistic healing? More importantly, how are schools preparing our youth for professions that offer alternative solutions to today's problems?

The figures appearing on the next three pages are followed by theoretical applications, which involve the use of the energy systems. There is a flow in each of these figures that depicts balance in the body. Our daily experiences play a role in determining the flow of energy in the body. There are two important points to keep in mind:

- Rhythmic entrainment, mindfulness and contemplative practices, and mental balance have the capacity to stabilize and center the body and create flow in the energy field.
- Fear, stress, fatigue, and judgment constrict the flow of energy because they cause stress on the adrenal system, resulting in a flight or fight response.

The figure below depicts the wireless electromagnetic flow of energy circulating in, around, and through the body. It depicts the energy flow that people may sense and experience when they meditation.

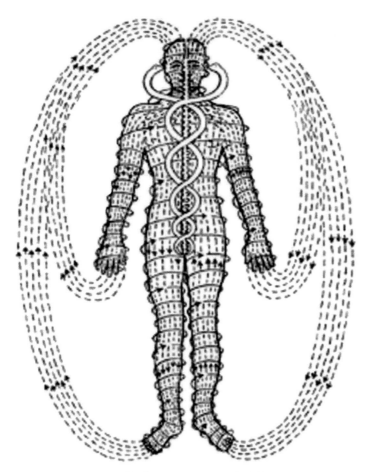

3 Caduceus energy field

We can experience relaxed, clear states of consciousness when we sense our body and being as energy. The scene "Our Natural Rhythms" demonstrates the process of stabilizing the energy body through contemplative practices such as yoga and trans drumming.

Harmonic frequencies are created through our thoughts and emotions and either attract or repel others. (When one newborn in the nursery begins to cry, for example, other babies follow suit.) Individuals who are highly sensitive to other peoples' energy (or "empaths") can feel "other people's feelings" in their body.

The following diagram shows the various energy fields surrounding the body sensed by energy workers, healers, and students I met at Omega teen camp.

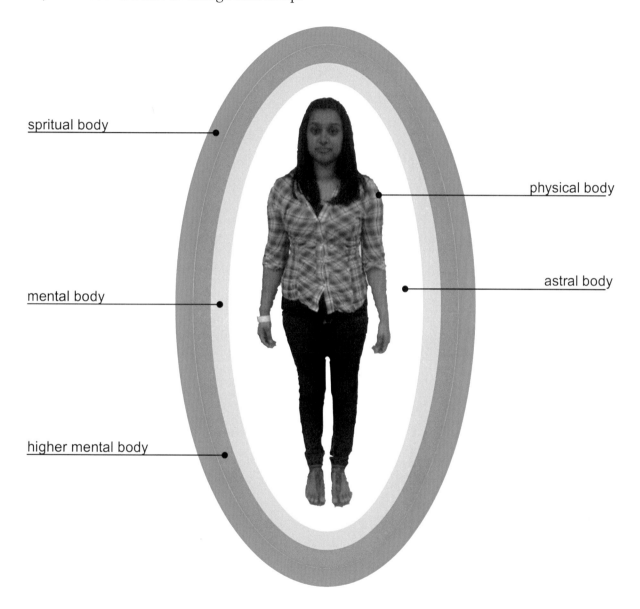

spritual body

physical body

mental body

astral body

higher mental body

4 Sayda modeling for the energy fields that surround the body.

The energy field, which surrounds the body, is seen above. Holistic practitioners such as acupuncturists, Reiki energy healers, and homeopaths all use healing modalities, which access or observe the body's energy, life force, or *prana*. These healing modalities cannot be measured with quantitative instruments; however, millions of people are using alternate therapies across the globe. How will these alternative healing modalities affect the professional training of our youth in the next decade with words like *Reiki*, *chakra*, and *energy meridian* becoming commonplace? Being open to belief systems from other cultures is one way to acknowledge and build bridges across cultures.

Diagram of energy meridians sensed by acupuncturists and chiropractors.

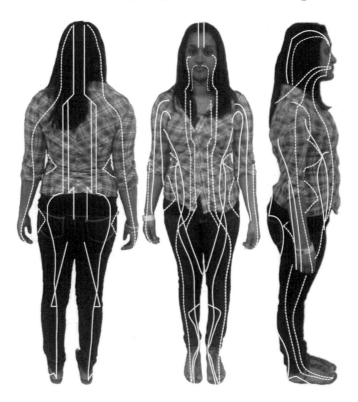

5- Sayda demonstrates the energy meridians

Vedic medicine teaches "the primary centers of consciousness are located in the upper brain and along the cerebra-spinal system, in the energy complexes of the chakras. Three main energy channels in the body connect the chakras. The primary energy channel, known as the Shushuma, travels up and down the spinal column. Two more channels travel through the chakras on either side, interweaving and creating a double helix of energy from the base of the spine to the crown. The Ida, or left channel, carries the feminine or lunar energy, and the right energy channel, or Pingala, carries the masculine or solar energy. There are said to be 72, 000 *nadis* or energy centers within the body/ mind but these carry the most voltage.

"… the chakras are represented visually by the lotus, which represents the gateway through which consciousness enters the world. The life vibration pulses out through thee power points, animating the mind and body" (Redmond CD). Redmond combines rhythmic entrainment from other cultures with Eastern contemplative practices to balance and align the energy centers in the body and increase awareness. The "unity" footage in the film was an experimental process using this system.

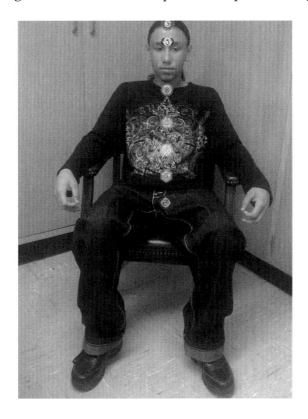

6 Carlos participating in mind up club at SHS (he loved the pictures of the chakras)

The Energy Centers, Archetypal Patterns and Personal Myths

Many teachers are concerned with the number of students who are lacking focus. As seen in the introduction of Dreaming New Schools, curriculum-driven teaching lends itself to disengagement from the learning process, and as a result "students in the US are bored, disinterested, distracted …from the learning process". Most learning, especially in secondary schools, is sedentary. It is not surprising that students have difficulty staying focused and are not interested in learning.

Energy Healers hold an awareness that emotions are directly related to the energy centers in the body. Emotionally driven archetypal patterns correlate to the energy centers in the body. In Jungian psychology, an inherited pattern of thought or symbolic imagery derived from the past collective experience and present in the individual unconscious are considered an archetype (dictionary.com). In other words, we allow our beliefs – correct or incorrect, consciously, or unconsciously -- to dictate our identities. These belief patterns have a tremendous impact on our perceptions, which then in turn affect our energy and our well-being. Physical illness results from an imbalance in the energy system. This imbalance is directly related to our core beliefs stored in cellular memory. (Myss, Dale-Lopez, Author). When negative beliefs are released and replaced with affirming beliefs, the individual creates an opportunity to experience a balanced flow of energy, resulting in healing. The image on the following page shows common archetypal characteristics that are stored in the energy centers.

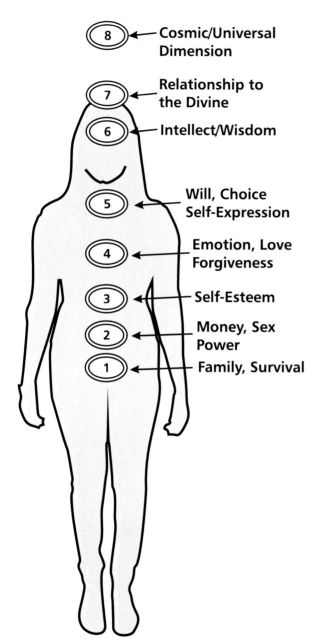

8 ←— Cosmic/Universal Dimension

7 ←— Relationship to the Divine

6 ←— Intellect/Wisdom

5 ←— Will, Choice Self-Expression

4 ←— Emotion, Love Forgiveness

3 ←— Self-Esteem

2 ←— Money, Sex Power

1 ←— Family, Survival

**7 Archetypal Images
Design by Paul Hoffman**

One teaching that is consistent in alternate healing methods is the importance of clearing one's energy field before and after a healing session, so the practitioner remains balanced. I developed the skill of becoming very sensitive to my own energy and the energies of others through continued practiced during my internship in the Light Body Training. When I open my field of energy to my light body, I can feel a clear path of light travel up my spine, cascading down from my heart to my crown and back down to my root. Sometimes when I chant, I can feel the light in my body expand outward and fill the room. I demonstrate this process during the film credits chanting, "Modah Ani". Steve Gorn plays solo on the flute at the end of the chant. I bow my head and inhale slowly, raising my head once again breathing in the soothing harmonics of the flute, thereby balancing my energy. I practice using my breath to balance my energy several times a day.

Improved Awareness, Improved Results

Educators and students would benefit tremendously by developing an awareness of the energy cycles in their body and the energy that other students bring into the classroom. I have seen a marked improvement in personal classroom management skills when I take time to notice these energy cycles and make the necessary adaptations to the lesson. Students can spin out of control when they are unaware of personal boundaries and/or energy patterns.

Body awareness can be an intrinsic part of learning at all age levels. As educators become aware of the energy cycles in the classroom, they can keep the class more engaged by introducing activities that will bring the students back in focus. This models self-awareness to their students. School schedules could include time for teachers to pause before instructional lessons throughout the day. This time could be used for staff and students to become more centered, balanced, present for one another and more engaged in learning. Guiding students to become mindful of their physical and emotional needs in the early years becomes a life-long skill. Children could be coached as early as primary school to recognize when their body needs movement, sound, or silence to help them to stay focused.

Bringing Body and Spirit into Focus

Educators can invigorate the energy body and grab their students' attention in several different ways. In "Our Natural Rhythms," in the film, I demonstrate how contemplative practices help align the body and its energy flow "by entrainment; using rhythm we can bring ourselves back to center again, and again, and again." The words "again, and again, and again" metaphorically demonstrate that entrainment is the process I use continually used to self-center.

I've used yoga postures, Donna Eden's energy meridian balancing, and breathing techniques in the classroom to help students become more aware of the energy in and around their bodies and to become more relaxed and focused. When I first introduced these ideas in the classroom, some students were reluctant, but most participated. Students who chose not to participate respected their peer's choice. Participating students enjoyed feeling more relaxed and comfortable in their bodies. Students used words like "it's so chill" to describe room D19.

Releasing Personal Myths

We allow our beliefs – correct or incorrect, consciously, or unconsciously -- to dictate our identities. These belief patterns have a tremendous impact on our perceptions, which then affect our energy and our well-being. Physical illness results from an imbalance in the energy system. This imbalance is directly related to our core beliefs stored in cellular memory. (Myss, Dale-Lopez, Author). When negative beliefs are released and replaced with affirming beliefs, the individual often experiences a balanced flow of energy, resulting in healing.

Myths often reinforce the established power structure. The late expert in mythology, Joseph Campbell, maintained that myths play a major role in defining the role of the individual. Clinical psychologist and specialist in energy psychology, David Feinstein, drew on Campbell's work to develop his perspectives in mythology and psychology.

Personal myths shape our belief systems and how we interact in the world. I like the way Feinstein describes personal myths in his forwarding address, as "the vibrant infrastructure that informs your life, whether or not you are aware of it" (Feinstein, lecture). Prevailing myths can be compared to the characters that we play in life, much like actors in a play. These myths have the potential to propel us into the creation of our future visions or disable us from experiencing growth and transformation.

Feinstein explains that myths "are rooted in biology, personal history, culture, and sacred sources" and can be used personally, socially, and culturally. Prevailing myths and their impact on systems changes with time. Feinstein states, "Mythology is grounded in the quintessential human ability to address the large questions of life through symbolism, metaphor, and narrative … Myths address the hunger to comprehend the natural world in a meaningful way; the search for a marked pathway through the succeeding epochs of human life; the need to establish secure and fulfilling

The film shows what can happen when the emotional and energy bodies are not in alignment. This was when I spontaneously discovered that I was part of the misunderstood learning community described in the film introduction and conclusion and story "The Good Enough Child" on page 37. The emotional release I expressed in the film reveals the process of me identifying and releasing a personal myth and the resulting limiting belief. There is an unfolding of a greater truth that reveals itself, I am innately loving, and lovable just as I am.

The film and book combined introduce a new mythology for learning, where personal transformation is possible, introducing holistic teaching models that engage the senses, such as the African American Tale and the Native American perspective on learning.

Holistic educational programs have been met with some controversy; however, I suggest that it is what is most needed during this tumultuous time in history. Holistic models integrating body, mind, and the animating force within all of us, meet the challenging needs of society.

relationships within a community; and the yearning to know one's part in the vast wonder and mystery of the cosmos" (Lecture).

Myths and the Educational System

I believe we have the potential to create a new myth concerning education and learning, translating our internal power into daily experiences that create inclusion, wholeness, joy, satisfaction, and learning through direct experience. Within this paradigm shift, I view learning as a relational experience where the student is invited to open to their innately creative intelligence as multi-dimensional beings. The child's emotional and innate intelligence is supported in an inclusive, supportive environment.

Mindfulness practices help us to become more self-aware and more responsive to our environment without attachment to the outcome of our perceived experiences. Scholars and pioneers in systems change and educational reform are offering clinically proved methods that help individuals practice self-empathy, self-awareness, and compassion for others. These practices are having a sustaining impact on the individual and their environment, interpersonally. Many schools are participating in programs that foster mindfulness and emotional intelligence initiated by pioneers like Jon Kabat Zinn, Goldie Hawn, Linda Lantieri, Parker Palmer, and Daniel Goldman, to name a few. Their programs include MBSR, the Inner Resilience Program, the Mind-Up Program, and teacher training like Parker Palmer's Courage and Renewal program. What a wonderful invitation to change our prevailing myths concerning learning and the institutions, which dictate the processes available to us. MBSR, Inner Resilience, and Mind Up are programs that students and teachers from the US and Canada are participating in. Programs like these support the emerging fields of harmonics, energy and consciousness. Healing and learning go hand in hand. Sound, rhythm and music are areas that can be explored through all disciplines in schools.

Children are naturally curious and interested in exploring their surroundings. But children learn through experience, and if their learning environment is not conducive to their authentic self – if, for example, a young child is constantly reprimanded for not being able to sit still in a traditional classroom – the myths that they absorb about themselves can have long-lasting, negative results.

Standardized testing is currently used as the *predominant* means to qualify intelligence, and the prevailing myth of the current educational system. Standards can be used as an inclusively support, tool to evaluate learning outcomes. We can realize the dreams of great men like Dr. Martin Luther King and Margaret Meade as we embark on creating a new mythology for learning, exploring, and being.

To be interested in learning, young adults must see that what they are learning is relevant to their lives. Boredom can lead to poor grades, which can lead to skipping class, and the spiral continues downward from there. What kind of myths is this student learning about *himself*?

Teaching to the test limits the teacher's autonomy to creatively explore curriculum. Educators are frustrated and start to believe negative myths about themselves.

What happens when students believe their negative self-talk? Administrators and "educators must address the reality that students are coming to school more depressed, angry, and fearful than in the past, and that they are acting on these impulses" (McCarthy 13). The many faculty, social workers, and administrators that I have worked with have noticed markedly increased incidents of stress, depression, and aggression among the student population.

The Darwinian model promoting a mindset of "me first!" rather than developing a mutually collective response to the needs of the 21st century supporting sustainability and growth for the global community has invasively affected our relationship to economic growth, education, leadership, politics, agriculture, and human relationships. Educators can

Studies support this hypothesis, citing increased incidence of binge drinking, carrying weapons, marijuana use, sexual activity, and drop-out rates (McCarthy, US Center for Disease Control). The increased incidence of single parent families is one factor that seems to have been overlooked when considering the impact of loss experienced by children.

teach youth to honor and cherish life by respectfully appreciating their differences. Participating in service projects that are relevant to student's interests and needs can support sustainable living. These projects will help students to believe in their own abilities and become more responsible as global citizens. This type of shift will have tremendous impact our future society, creating a positive cycle of learning and giving. I envision schools developing integrative, transformative curriculum following holistic models, not just teaching students to ace a standardized test, but supporting respect and care for the whole community of life, for ecological integrity and for social and economic justice.

When developing programs that foster self-direction and positive action, we ask the questions expressed in the film: "Who am I? What do I want? Where am I going? And how do I get there?" Curriculum that empowers the child to reach his or her unique potential evolving consciousness emotionally, intellectually, and physically provides crucial elements needed in school programs today. This curriculum will encourage youth to appreciate themselves in "other ways of knowing" (Broomfield). Discovering "other ways of knowing" helps students recognize commonalities among belief systems, dismantling the fears resulting from ignorance or lack of experience.

Learning becomes transformational. Compassion, tolerance, creativity, and ingenuity become the cornerstones for excellence. These qualities naturally thrive by mindfully exploring our emotional and creative intelligences through the arts, music, nature, and contemplative practices. Learning becomes relevant to the experience of the moment, with a keen interest in supporting and sustaining the whole in this growth process. In short, we evolve. In July of 2009 I participated in a Sasquatch adventure with dolphin expert, Joan Ocean and a small group of journey folk.

I'd been facilitating cultural diversity courses to our High School staff that year and reluctantly agreed to join the Sasquatch adventure after recognizing that my fears were masking personal bias I had against extra-terrestrial beings. I've always believed in the possibility of life forms on other planets or from other dimensional realities, but I had no in exploring what that might mean for me personally or for humanity at large.

Then I had an "ah ha" moment! How could I be in integrity and model mutuality and acceptance with my co-workers, with my own fears and bias'. I felt hypocritical to encourage my peers to examine their fears and prejudice with my own bias against life forms which I knew nothing about?

Joan patiently listened as I expressed my fears and encouraged me to follow my inner guidance. I am grateful Joan reassured me that it was indeed safe, to say yes to the exquisite experience of embracing the unknown. And I was amazed to be blissfully showered in beams of unconditional love when I asked Grandmother Haloti to show me her relationship to humanity, and our beloved planet, earth.

Now, back to how this may apply to schools…Urban schools with extremely diverse populations can be models for teaching tolerance to schools with homogeneous populations. All schools face the challenge of creating safe environments and treating **all** members of the learning community with dignity and respect. Many students in urban schools come from families that are first- or second-generation immigrants. These families are often steeped in cultural and ritual practices. *Understanding the religious and cultural practices of our students offers an opportunity to teach tolerance, acceptance, and ultimately appreciation of diversity if approached with awareness and sensitivity by administrative and teaching staff.* Inviting students and their families to school events to honor diversity and celebrate their cultures is a wonderful way to build community. Seeking commonalities between cultures can help parents and students overcome fears that may come up when they are exposed to ideas that are foreign to them.

The Creative Process of Personal Transformation

Figure 8 is an illustration of the creative process leading to personal transformation. It can be used as a tool to interpret the creative process of personal transformation. Although the diagram is flat, I suggest you imagine it as a three-dimensional, holographic moving spiral demonstrating the continual movement and growth, which occurs during the process of creativity.

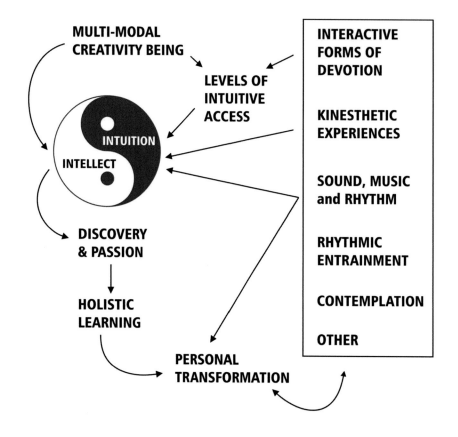

8 Creative Process of Personal Transformation
(Second Core Faculty Evaluation of Thesis, Spring 2005 designed by Paul Hoffman 2013)

In the CPPT, human beings are understood to be Multi-Modal Creative Beings (Cedillos). A multimodal being is constantly in the act of creating. We have the capacity to access our creative intelligence on a variety of levels, but this process requires balanced use of the intellect and without attachment to any **one** specific medium (i.e., contemplation, dance, drumming, jogging, meditation, yoga, writing, or other forms of expressive art.) (See above figure).

I choose the yin yang form to visually represent the need for balance between intellect and intuition to support personal development. The relationship between intellect and intuition is a creative process.

In the CPPT, discovery and passion bring joy to the learning experience, which renews interest in learning and resulting in personal growth and transformation. In the CPPT, the multi-modal being continues to develop through personal awareness by experiencing themselves actively engaging in various mediums, or processes, bringing joy and inspiration. In my case, some of these mediums included mindful meditation, silence, sound, and rhythm.

The mediums that bring passion and joy vary in each individual and are not limited to the arts. This model acknowledges that all mediums have the potential to inspire, are not fixed in time, and therefore, promote individual continuing growth, with conscious intent.

Interaction with the CPPT

Creativity inspires growth and expansion. There is an in-breath as well as an out-breath in this process. Between the two breaths is the pause, where the creative spirit beholds its potential for growth. In the silence, or void, everything exists simultaneously in its unexpressed form. If the CPPT is viewed as a holographic spiral, the beginning and end of the creative process flows cyclically, as one complete unit. What seems like the end of a learning cycle may be the beginning of a more comprehensive thought form.

This process can be compared to the enlightened moments of realization that steer the seeker's path towards self-actualization and transformation (transcendence) as seen in Abraham Maslow's hierarchy of needs. Maslow explains; man's physiological needs, safety needs, need for belonging, and need for esteem must occur before the ultimate process of self-actualization can begin. Maslow is a well-known psychologist whose theory of human needs had a major impact on psychology, as we know it today. "What is not commonly known is that Maslow's pyramidal hierarchy was not topped by self-actualization. The final layer of the pyramid has been censored in the mainstream Universities in the West. Maslow's hierarchy ends with transcendence…or …wisdom of the soul" (Blanc 40). Maslow's hierarchy actually supports transformative learning. Personal transformation is demonstrated by the multi-modal creative being engaging in the creative process, which results in learning. I call this process "transformative learning."

CPPT Research Format

This text demonstrates just one learner's journey through the creative process. Sound, rhythm, and music are the sensory mediums that *I* used as teaching tools for transformative learning, to focus my intellect, access my intuition, enhance my creative spirit, and ultimately bring joy and life to my learning process.

I use descriptive narratives in the text to describe my research process. These narratives support contributing theories and wisdom teachings, which inspired the conceptualization and production of the film available on my website, dreamingnewschools.com.

The narratives in Dreaming New Schools show my intuitive and intellectual process of discovery. In this process, I become the objective observer, observing my response to the immediate circumstance, and maintaining focus by listening to my body's response to the circumstance. They demonstrate the balance of intellect and creativity within a unified whole as depicted in the CPPT. They are an integral part of the Art-based Heuristic research process used in this text and in my doctoral thesis. These narratives describe my experiences with sound, rhythm, music, and energy, resulting in personal transformation as a marked change for the better.

The process of transformative learning can be challenging but is well worth the effort. Transformative learning requires decomposition much like nature, where organic material breaks down and changes form. In transformative learning, the individual's beliefs and their approach to life experiences also changes, moving towards wholeness. "This 'deep level of learning' challenges existing and taken for-granted assumptions, notions, and meanings of what learning is about" (Dirkx 125). Because this mode of learning is cyclical, it continues to shift and expand. "Learning that is transformative "redirects and re-energizes those who pause to reflect on what their lives have been and take on new purposes and perspectives" (McWhinney, Markos 16).

I experienced a paradigm shift within myself while I was researching my theories. Within this process, my perspective changed from looking outward to receive my inspiration from other teachers and musicians, to looking inward, and becoming inspired through my personal experience of creating. When I introduced the idea of learning being an art form, to my students, they became comfortable stretching beyond their comfort zone, exploring new ways of learning and presenting the work they'd learned to their peers. I saw how important it was to encourage students to kindle their inner-spark and become self- directed, self- motivated creative learners. I continue to shift as I remain open to the idea of expanding my consciousness seeing every day as a new beginning, and every moment of every day ripe with opportunity for growth.

Self-Direction as a Means to an End ... Or a New Beginning?

In 2000, I took on an enormous project and went back to school to earn my Ph.D. I was working full time and raising my three teens as a single parent, and although this project pales in comparison with the ongoing responsibilities and learning experiences of parenthood, I discovered some wonderful things about myself, and my learning process through my studies.

I chose Union Institute for my Ph.D. program because I felt they were really on to something in terms of offering self-directed Ph.Ds. As parents we hope our children become self-directed, lifelong learners and creative problem solvers. However, there are not many Ph.D. programs that allow students such freedom, and I felt it was a perfect match for me.

During my studies, I made two firm commitments to myself: To honor my learning style, and to allow my learning process to evolve. I did my best to offer the same opportunity for my students. With the help of my wonderful advisors, I planned an amazing program, integrating field research, in travels to India and Peru, attending seminars in the US with teachers and healers from many cultures through peer days and using more traditional research methods. I learned much during my studies and was eager to inspire my students to discover their own unique talents and abilities.

I was honoring my own learning style and loving every moment of it – until my last semester, when disappointment hit me hard.

The University changed their program requirements to maintain accreditation from the Board of Regents, and things got messy. I found myself without a doctoral committee a month before graduation. My core faculty advisors left, along with several other professors who were leaders in the arts and creative studies. Suddenly, my support system was gone. The changes in Union's program presented by the Board of Regents had a major impact on my thesis, which delayed my graduation by a year. In a nutshell, I was asked to use a linear format to model a non-linear process. The short film I'd written and produced "Using Multicultural Sound as a Tool for Creativity, Contemplation, and Personal Transformation" accompanied by a two-hundred pages of contextual essays was no longer considered my thesis. This created confusion for me personally and professionally. I ultimately rewrote my thesis to comply with the new direction that Union Institute decided to take.

What keeps our internal spark alive with hope, even when we are met with adversary? Before Union's huge academic restructuring, I had confidence knowing that my vision of scholarly research was respected and supported by my faculty advisors and doctoral committee. No doubt, losing my connections at the University has had its challenges.

On a positive note, my studies, seminars, and internships changed my life and expanded my perceptions of relatedness. I am grateful to the individuals who shared their hearts, minds, souls, and cultural perspectives, which have helped me become a better person.

Students seldom hear that what we consider failure is part of all great endeavors. Being a student while I was teaching opened my eyes to entirely new perspectives. I could relate to my high school students on a whole new level through our shared experience as learners exploring creative ways to solve problems. My students appreciated this. On a deeper lever, I discovered the multi-faceted opportunities for self-exploration, growth and healing as the Multi-Dimensional Creative Being that I understand myself to be.

Chapter Three

"We are not walking in the shadow of our ghosts,
We are alive in our passion."
Babba Maal, ***One Giant Leap***

Principle Two: We have the Potential to Access Information and Gain Wisdom on Many Creative Levels

I've come to understand that information and deep levels of awareness are available to us in many forms. Slowing down enough to be fully present opens our natural ability to access our inner wisdom. In my internship trainings, I learned to experience subtle energies.

When I originally wrote this chapter, my focus was directed on how sound, rhythm, and music could be used specifically for personal transformation. In this section, I share some of the intuitive practices that have graciously guided me towards becoming the Multi-Dimensional Creative Being that I experience myself as today.

Music and the CPPT

In his work *Music, the Brain and Ecstasy*, scientist, author, and musical composer Robert Jourdain addresses the theme of music and creativity. At 18 months, infants begin to sing spontaneously, the same as infant babbling, which occurs somewhat earlier. Parents respond to the babbling, and it goes on to become speech; they ignore the singing, and it stops (Jourdain 188). Musicality flourishes when it is reinforced at an early age.

Musical composition purely expresses the composer's creative spirit no matter what the composition sounds like, as Jourdain explains, "integral to the modern notion of musical talent is the idea that everyone is born to compose" (186). Students draw pictures, write stories, create architectural structures, and design scientific experiments. Musical training in school is most often accomplished by learning to play an instrument or singing composed music rehearsed in a choral group. Students are *not* expected to compose their own music.

Inviting students to creatively engage in the composition of music opens an opportunity for them to experience their creativity. Students learn to value the process of cultivating creativity. They may even experience the healing qualities of music more intimately, especially if they sing the music they compose.

In the film, we see that composing music isn't limited to trained musicians. As Rosanne Ranari states: "Music is spontaneous […] it transcends the boundaries that place limitations." The film can be used as an inspirational tool help teachers and students become more comfortable trying new skills. I really enjoyed creating the little tunes I sang in Dreaming New Schools. Creativity becomes the learning process!

Being More Present

Contemplative practices like mindful meditation, vocalizing and yoga cultivate an awareness of the connection between body and mind. These practices have a cumulative effect on our presence and awareness. In a relaxed state our mind chatter takes a back seat, and we begin to experience being more fully present.

Scientific evidence proves that there is a correlation between the brain waves and the state of consciousness: "Research projects in major universities have explored the neurophysiology of meditation, deep relaxation states, and mind/body interactions during healing. In one study, a simple meditation technique used 20 minutes a day caused profound changes in blood pressure, stress handling ability, immune response, and feelings of wellbeing" (Thompson neuroacoustics.com).

How cool is this? "[…] sound frequency patterns built into the music have been shown clinically to cause positive changes in consciousness and brain wave function" and "coordinating of right/left brainwave activity and general slowing of brainwave activity which is associated with deep relaxation, stress reduction, creativity, insight, and problem solving" (Thompson neuroacoustics.com).

In other words, learning experiences could potentially be transformed if students and faculty were given active opportunities to engage in the deeper, subtle healing qualities of music and sound and other art forms as part of their curriculum. Through deeper exploration of sound and music, students and staff could first-handedly experience their unique capacity to feel more at peace, more focused, more relaxed, and more creative! These are skills that would benefit all participants who are exposed to the fast-paced, overcrowded stresses of public schools. (In fact, one of my students came to this conclusion at a writing conference she attended with me in 2008. I share her story in the final chapter of this book.)

When a content area is mindfully explored, the body's senses become alive with awareness that is actually stored in the body as memory. I took a course, which was team taught by cellular biologist Bruce Lipton, and expert in Somatic studies, Susan Apoyshan, at Naropa University in 2003. The Biology of Belief was chock full of scientific information on cellular memory. Bruce shared with wonderful visuals, stories and research practices and Susan helped us integrate the information into our bodies through visualizations and movement. I lost my notebook at the end of the week and was really disappointed (good teacher / student that I was). You can imagine how surprised I was, when six months later I shared much of what I had learned about cellular memory and learning in a child development class with detailed clarity.

Although sound, rhythm, and music are the mediums that I used to explore growth and transformation, the mediums that support intuitive growth are as vast as the individual exploring the medium itself! It's the end result -- the transformative process – that we want to encourage. How the student comes to that result is a personal choice.

Consciousness and Intent

"Your consciousness is your energy of attention and intention at any given time. Your consciousness is reflected in the emotions that play across both the surface and depth of your experience. Your consciousness is your awareness of you as an essential spark within the fabric of creation. Your consciousness is the representation of you as if taken in snapshots from moment to moment." - Yosama Challenor, M.D.

The way we approach the use of practices such as sound, rhythm, music, and other artistic mediums has an impact on the learning experience. Consciously directing our intention towards healing and transformation is an important aspect of this process. Schools and their students, faculty, and administrators have an opportunity for growth, transformation, and deep change – but only if they recognize the opportunity for what it is and work

The cyclical order and flow of the film represents my perception of the creative process as the artist-researcher, film producer, traveler, student, musician, interviewer, performer, and teacher. Its focus and reference are transmutable, much like the photons that shift from wave to particle. Like the CPPT, which moves in a spiral the outcome of the creative process of producing the film was unpredictable.

towards a specific goal. This requires an increased, focused consciousness on the part of students *and* faculty!

Transformative learning is experiential. Transformative learning has a lot to do with intent and cultivating self-awareness. It requires developing keen observation skills, recognition of emotional blockages, and some level of emotional detachment from the experience as it is encountered. In other words, we recognize that our emotions are simply an expression of ourselves, that we are much more than our emotions. You can see this in the conclusion of the film, when I followed my intuition sharing what was most alive for me at that moment. I was as surprised at what came out as you probably will be if you watch the film to its completion. continued I wanted to be "really great at one thing, so I could make a difference in the world". The little girl inside of me didn't believe she was good enough to be sharing such an intimate notion. Minutes later I felt an impulse to sit in front of the camera once again and share the next personal awareness that came through in the form of a stream of consciousness. I didn't realize that in that moment my perception of not being good enough was about to shift. "What I didn't realize was that I was really great at something. I was great at being me." What a great learning that was!!

Sensitivity and Children

While we're talking about working on different intuitive levels, I'd like to touch on the subject of sensitive children.

Thoughts and words are powerful. Words have an emotional stigma or value attached to them by the person using the word and the subculture in which they have been raised. "Sensitivity" is one such word. One understanding of the word *sensitive* would be "having perception through the senses." Perhaps the more common view of sensitivity has to do with being "easily hurt or annoyed." What do statements like "She's being overly sensitive" mean? Who, or what, is she or he being overly sensitive towards?

And who is to say where "acceptable" levels of sensitivity leave off and "overly" sensitive behaviors begin? Many of these "sensitive students"

Sensitive children may be considered weak or lacking the courage to withstand pain or injury, particularly in environments where there are large numbers of students or strong viewpoints that are critical, domineering or survival based. These children can well up with emotions, confounding both parent and teacher. Other children "toughen up" (or shut down and deny their emotions) to fit in or avoid experiencing pain. I fit into the second category. Like many sensitive children, in time, I learned to "toughen up" so that others around me would not feel so uncomfortable.

Most adults feel uncomfortable around challenging emotions. We qualify our emotions, rather than expressing them without judgment. We view happy as "good," while being sad, depressed, anxiousness, or overwhelmed are considered "bad." When negative feelings are expressed in a safe environment, there's room for growth and change. Expressing our feelings when they rise unlocks them from our subconscious and can even release them from our body and its memory of the pain they caused. An increased interest in alternative healing therapies gives testament to this idea, which I have experienced first-hand many times.

What many parents and teachers may not understand is that sensitive children have highly developed perceptual skills. They can sense other people's emotions at a deep level although they may not be able to express these sensations. These children are masters at reading non-verbal communication skills and often "sensing the energies round them, which are projected from feelings and thought forms of others! This sensitivity can be overwhelming, and sensitive children often have difficulty in large groups, or loud groups, because they have not developed the skill of setting safe boundaries. They can literally *feel* the thoughts, emotions, and energy put out by others, which affects their sense of equilibrium. We see them fidgeting, distracted, agitated, or overwhelmed. While all children prefer experiential learning activities, sensitive children are extremely kinesthetic. They come to understand the world through engagement and experience. Sitting at a desk for hours on end, filling out worksheets so that they can earn points simply does not make sense. Boredom or overwhelm sets in, followed soon after by misbehavior or "tuning out".

Guiding children in understanding that we have an etheric field of energy surrounding our bodies is a helpful tool they can access in learning to maintain safe boundaries. There are simple ways to clear one's energy field, and energy hygiene is an important concept for children of all ages to learn. Even young children will understand this concept of beginning the cleansing process by imagining or visualizing their own etheric field filled with white light. With practice, this skill becomes second nature in time. This will help the more sensitive child to maintain balance and clarity.

"The etheric body (from "ether," the state between energy and matter) is composed of tiny energy lines-- "like a sparkling web of light beams" -- similar to the lines on a television screen. It has the same structure as the physical body including all the anatomical parts and all the organs.

I've witnessed an increased awareness and sensitivity among my students when they are given the opportunity to still their minds and feel a sense of harmony as their bodies. Creating intentional time and space in the school environment promotes this awareness naturally. Sensitivity can be viewed in a new light.

Respecting the Individuality of All Students

When schools support our uniquely individual creative expressions, children grow up confident being who they are. I spent my entire childhood trying to fit into a model that did not support my own growth process or learning style. It took a Ph.D. and a relentless internal drive to reach this conclusion. Self- acceptance, much like self- awareness, is a process. The sages compare it to the peeling of an onion. This process requires release, patience, non-judgment, and gentle action.

The story below demonstrates this process. *When I first wrote this short story, it became an entry-point to a meditation, which I experienced in my body as I was writing it, like a shamanic journey of sorts.*

The Good Enough Child

Once there was a child who was born through a tunnel of light. She came to visit the world of the known and the unknown.

As she traveled through this tunnel, she thought to herself, "I am good enough as I am, I am good enough as I am, as I am, as I am" and she whirled, and she swirled, and the tunnel of light became a tunnel of darkness and dampness, and she heard voices all around her saying things about her.

"Her nose was too big", "no it was too flat", they argued, and her legs were so gangly, and her skin was so wrinkly. "She looks like her father – no she looks like her mother!" they shouted, it seemed though their thoughts were barely a whisper in the hospital room, so clean and antiseptically white.

Each criticism felt like an arrow wedged in her little heart. She tried hard to remember "I am good enough, I am good enough, I am good enough as I am, as I am, as I am." And she did for a while.

As time went by, the child became a young girl. Although her body was small, her heart was enormously tender and true. She understood much and felt the pain of her friends and family when they were sad or lonely.

Her family and friends, who did not understand her kindliness, often teased the little girl. "She's so sensitive!" they exclaimed. "Why do her eyes well up so easily? Why can't she be STRONG?"

The words spoken felt like daggers wedged in her heart. She pushed the feeling way down deep, until the dagger was no longer seen, and no longer felt. Once again, she tried to remember, I am good enough just as I am, I am good enough just as I am as I am as I am, as I am," but this time the words became jumbled in her mind, spinning furiously around, making confusing sounds. "Am I? Am I? Am I enough? Am I just? Am I good? Am I? Am I? Am I?" And for the first time, she wondered, "Who am I? What is my purpose, she asked herself?" For she had indeed forgotten.

Many years went by, and the child became a young woman. These were lonely years, often filled with confusion, as she knew deep down that there was more to life than schooling, and cleaning, and preparing for this or that. She missed the little child who was good enough just as she was, good enough just as she was, as she was, as she was.

Her days were busy with activity, and she had forgotten how to see and hear the child who was born through the tunnel of light.

On occasion, she would place an owl feather she was given when she was a young girl under her pillow, hoping to re-member. And on occasion, the child who was born through the tunnel of light would visit the young woman in her dreams, to help her remember that she was, indeed one and the same: "I am good enough as I am, as I am, as I am."

Still, the young woman yearned to feel in her bones, that she was good enough, and to know that she was indeed good enough just as she was.

One day, the young woman went for a walk in the woods, singing sweetly to the trees and the animals as she made her way along. As she walked, she came upon a huge rock lying close to a tree. She sat on the rock and closed her eyes to listen to the woods more closely. Down, down, down she drifted to the world beneath the earth, where her shadows lived. She was frightened at first, for the underworld is dark and deep, and her eyes had grown dim over the years. She could not see as clearly as she did as a child.

The young woman felt for her owl feather in her pocket and called to owl to guide and protect her on her journey. Soon, she felt the ruffle of owl feathers on her brow, and sensed Owl's piercingly protective eyes upon her. Owl was bestowing wisdom to the young woman, and she felt comfort in his presence.

As frightened as she was, the young woman did not try to escape her fears. And she knew that there was something REALLY BIG, and REALLY IMPORTANT for her to see in the deep, dark recesses of the underworld, something that would not, or even could not, *be seen in the world above, so down, down, down she went in the recesses of her mind to unlock the key to her happiness.*

The first layer of forest was damp, with gnarly vines. There was a layer of green growth, like the web of the spider that she had to walk through to continue her descent. She felt creepy, crawly things beneath her feet, and they sent chills up her spine. Still, the young woman walked, for she knew that the answer to her question was deeper, still.

At the end of the web, she was taken through a tunnel of wind where the wind was breath, but the breath did not move. She felt her lungs collapse in fear as the air was squeezed out of her body. She knew by these feelings that she was closer still to her answer, so deeper she went, into the "no air," and into the darkness she fell until it enveloped her being. As she became the darkness, she saw a shimmer of light, like a shiny metal inside her body. It was wedged inside her heart, like a dagger.

Her hand reached into a violet-blue flame, to feel the dagger, and she felt its sting and as she reached, she understood that it was she who had placed the dagger in her own heart, by forgetting that she was "good enough".

With that realization, the dagger shattered into a million pieces and disappeared into the darkness. As the dagger began to break, she felt her body being led by a large group of angels to the upper world, where rainbow colors in every shade of luminosity shined through her being.

The young woman became a lady that day and held the key to her heart in her hand, placing it gently where it belonged. I am free, I am whole, I am enough she said to herself. And she is! (Wink)

9 Volcano Irazu National Park Costa Rica Feb 2010

Chapter Four

"That which we witness, we are forever changed by, and once witnessed, we can never go back."
Angeles Arrien

Principle Three: Using Intellect and Intuition Creates Balance

As I made a personal commitment to explore my intuitive and cognitive skills to the best of my ability, I honored my unique learning style. I became more aware of my creative process as a result. Something really interesting happened when I was writing my contextual essay, or PDE (which is basically what Union Institute calls a doctoral thesis). I was meditating daily and following my intuition supporting my sense of body awareness and creative flow. I used music to self-center and inspire my creativity. I'd been integrating the energy work I'd learned and experiencing the subtle energetic flows in my body, in other people and in nature. I'd read over two hundred books and articles, highlighting, and dog-earing the pages where facts and ideas that were most important to my study were located. The week I'd set aside to begin writing my PDE, I was woken up in the middle of the night for several nights in a row. It felt like the right time to write for some reason. I'd had an organized list of the topics I'd be writing about to direct my course, (an outline of sorts, derived from the mind map I've included in chapter 8), and I began writing, organically in a free form stream of consciousness. A voice inside my mind began informing me of the citations to use, as references, by page number and title of book or name of author in some cases. Each time I referred to the book or article, I saw that it was dog-eared, highlighted, or had very specific relevance to the topic at hand. This continued for several weeks, until I my work on the original draft was complete. It felt like a download of information specifically designed for its purpose, congruent and free flowing. I did not use note cards or any of the techniques that our high school students were taught to use in English Literature or composition classes to prepare for their state regents in writing my two-hundred-page contextual essay. Imagine what I might have accomplished had I been encouraged to open to my creative impulse as a young child? More importantly, imagine how many children would benefit today from this opportunity!

Spiritual and Emotional Intelligence

Spiritual intelligence is revered throughout the world in religions and spiritual traditions of indigenous cultures. Research in consciousness, meditation, visualization, and contemplative practices are becoming more common and, as a result, more valued in various cultures and settings. By exploring the highly creative and intuitive aspects of our intelligence – those areas where boundaries are not clearly defined -- we get a clearer picture of what we're all capable of. Cultivating Spiritual Intelligence is a powerful means for identifying highly creative approaches to problem-solving and value-based transformative learning.

Can we increase our spiritual perceptiveness, and why would we want to do so? Dana Zohar and Dr. Ian Marshall's research indicates that "through a more cultivated use of our Spiritual Intelligence, and through personal honesty and courage that such cultivation requires, we can find deeper meanings within ourselves, and we can use that reconnection with the deeper sources to serve causes and processes much larger than ourselves" (Zohar, Marshall 17). In other words, if we can connect with that spiritual side, not only will we benefit, but those around us will, too.

Zohar and Marshall's define Spiritual Intelligence as "the intelligence with which we address and solve problems of meaning and value" (Zohar, Marshall 4), and "the intelligence with which we can place our actions and our lives in a wider, richer, meaning-giving context" (Zohar Marshall 4). Zohar and Marshall maintain "neither the IQ or EQ (Emotional Intelligence), separate or in combination, allows us to explain the full complexity of human intelligence, nor the vast richness of the human soul and imagination" (Zohar, Marshall 5). Simply stated, we are all much more than our IQ, our EQ, or even the two of these numbers combined. It's who we are inside – that part of us that ironically cannot be measured – that displays our gifts, whether they are academic or something else entirely. It will come as no surprised that this tends to be overlooked in

Educational Psychologist Howard Gardener's foundation for teaching multiple intelligences gained enough momentum to infiltrate teacher training in public schools in the 1990's, although it didn't sustain itself due to the radical shift towards standardized testing as a means of authentic assessment.

How many of Gardner's multiple intelligences can you spot in the film?

the public school system! However, "no one would dispute that schools should prepare young people to be empathetic, responsible, motivated citizens who manage their emotions and develop lasting relationships" (McCarthy 13).

As educators, we are dealing with a wounded population and are overwhelmed by the consequences of this tragedy. Educators can be given opportunity to teach from more balanced perspectives offers opportunities for students to find meaning through learning. Educators can utilize learning processes, which facilitate increased faculties of the intellect, body, mind, and creative spirit. I see the full development of our creativity as a natural part of conscious evolution.

Holism Requires Balance

Intelligence plays an important role in understanding human behavior; however, it is through creativity that we can understand the human ability to cope with challenging situations in novel and appropriate ways. Leading scholars and scientists such as Deepak Chopra, Carolyn Myss, Fred Alan Wolfe, Wolf Singer, Ken Wilber, Gregg Braden, Brian Josephson, and Jon Kabat Zinn, share common theories based on Spiritual Intelligence which suggest that human beings are only scratching the surface of our potential. Ken Wilber describes spirituality as "levels of consciousness that perceive or intuit the vast wholeness and meaning of the cosmos, wholeness unfathomable in terms of material reality, personal identity, or cultural identity" (Miller13). Educational leaders in the holistic movement such as Ron Miller and Rachel Kessler stress the importance of teaching children to become authentic, compassionate human beings who respect their own individuality.

There is great benefit for creating balance between technological, scientific, and holistic models of education. The challenge before us is to create school systems that behave systemically while supporting holism. Educators who make attempts to bring creativity into the classroom are doing so AGAINST ALL ODDS, rather than being supported by the very system in which they belong. The amount of energy this requires is daunting (if you've seen films dealing with these issues, such as ***Freedom Writers***, then you know what I'm talking about). But when the system supports authentic communication, authentic leadership, and authentic learning, holism is a natural byproduct.

Spiritual Intelligence (the animating force within all of creation) also supports personal transformation, bringing transformative learning experiences to the forefront of our educational institutions. The traditional educational model provides only a partial understanding of change, self-discovery, and social criticism. All children are special, and to classify or segregate them creates shame and division. Inspiring each child to reach his or her own unique potential will serve our youth with greater clarity, joy, and authenticity. If educational leaders recognize the many ways in which we demonstrate our intelligence, we can encourage each child to explore their unique talents and potential. We can inspire children to become self-aware, self-directed visionaries -- skills that will help to promote what Zohar calls "servant leaders, or someone who is responsible for bringing higher vision and value to others by showing them how to use it" (Zohar, Marshall 16).

Theoretical Basis for Spiritual Intelligence (For Scientific Minds)

Spiritual Intelligence is based on the brain's third neural system, the synchronous neural oscillations that unify data across the whole brain. "This process unifies, integrates, and has the potential to transform material arising from the other two processes." "It facilitates a dialog between reason and emotion, between mind, and body" (Zohar 7). I find it very interesting that individuals who have cultivated a deep sense of spiritual awareness (or spiritual intelligence) such as Dr. Martin Luther King, the Dali Lama, Amritananadamayi Devi, (Amma)or Thich Nhat Hanh are greatly respected by academics, yet the topic of spirituality can still be quite awkward to address in an experiential manner!

While Spiritual Intelligence has been awkward for academics to investigate because existing science is not equipped to study things that cannot be objectively measured, a great deal of scientific evidence for Spiritual Intelligence does exist (Zohar). In the 1990's, neuro-the late, psychologist, Michael Persinger, Ph.D. laid groundwork for researching Spiritual Intelligence. Then in 1997, Neurologist V.S. Ramachandran and his team at the University of California researched the existence of the "God Spot" on the brain, noting: "This built-in spiritual center is located among neural connections in temporal lobes of the brain. On scans taken with positron emission topography, these neural areas light up whenever research subjects are exposed to religious or spiritual discussions" (Zohar 11). In the past, this work has been linked to mystical experiences of people who used hallucinogenic drugs such as LSD. Ramachandran's work is the first to demonstrate activity in the "God Spot" without drug use! "This demonstrates that the brain has evolved to ask, 'ultimate questions', to have and to use sensitivity to a wider meaning and value" (Zohar 12). Continued neuro-scientific research in mindfulness indicates that several parts of the brain light up during meditation, creating positive responses biochemically in the body and in the brain itself (8th annual conference in MBSR, U Mass).

Austrian Neurologist Wolf Singer demonstrated a neural process in the brain called the binding problem, which is devoted to unifying and giving meaning to our experience. Singer's work on serial neural connections is the basis for the IQ, allowing the brain to think logically and rationally, step by step. Our neural network organization is the basis for our EQ. He equates these processes to the two most prevalent types of computers -- serial computers and parallel computers. Both can perform the primary functions of serial and network organizers, but neither computer program can search for deeper meaning and ask *why*. They simply process information. **Spiritual Intelligence is the bridge between all processes of the body and mind.**

Integrity and Honesty

Learning to be critical thinkers requires integrity – a real confidence -- in observing one's belief systems. Our thinking extends beyond self-inquiry to support and facilitate social change. As cultural anthropologist Angeles Arrien suggests, observing our thoughts and emotions without judgment could be extremely beneficial to the entire learning community. Clearer understanding and acceptance of our present state of mind encourages more authentic interactions with others. **Imagine not being afraid to give an opinion without being shy or defensive about it, or simply being comfortable enough in your own skin – and mind – to say, "I don't know."** When authentic interactions become a part of our daily practice, they have the potential to bring greater integrity to our daily encounters. And I say hooray for Emotional Intelligence.

Emotional Intelligence a can become an integral part of teacher training. Emotional Intelligence can be cultivated in primary education and continued in secondary education in under-served communities where students are met with unusually high levels of stress in their lives. It may help children who suffer from distractibility by fostering self-acceptance. Once children feel accepted as uniquely creative, they can begin to practice the self-regulating skills necessary to become focused, authentic human beings.

Chapter Five

"At the center of non-violence stands the principle of love."
Dr. Martin Luther King Jr.

Principle Four: Learning Holistically Supports Growth and Transformation

What is transformative learning, and why is it so important? Jack Mezirow, a pioneer in education reform, depicts transformative learning as a process, effecting change in a point of reference (Mezirow 15). These points of reference are primarily the result of cultural assimilation and the idiosyncratic influences of primary caregivers. During adolescence, young adults begin questioning these points of reference. We are at choice to further develop the validity of our points of reference, determining whether they reflect our personal truth as incoming information and new experiences are presented to us.

Transformation Through Holism

The traditional academic learning model stresses only a partial understanding of the process of change, self-discovery, and social criticism. Holistic education, on the other hand, emphasizes the importance of the whole and the interdependence of its parts. In fact, the root of the word *holism* refers to the aspect of being complete, as in complete systems. Holistic education provides a learning model where students become more aware of universal, interconnected relationships. In this process, they have

In the film, Dreaming New Schools, *UCLA graduate and Transpersonal Psychologist Marcia Dale Lopez explains: "Concepts are always changing, and who we are is always changing." Increased awareness of life-affirming changes fosters self-acceptance and love. As teachers view their shortcomings as opportunities for growth, students will learn through their example.*

the opportunity to see *themselves* as part of a unified whole and understand that their actions have an effect on that whole.

A holistic approach to teaching offers opportunity for transformative learning, or "learning from the inside out," a process grounded in a more intuitive and emotional sense of our experiences, creating opportunity for imaginative and personal ways of knowing (Dirkx, Miller 79). To sustain a holistic approach supporting personal transformation within the learning community, administrators and educators take the role of servant leader, creating nurturing learning environments where student and teacher feel safe to explore more personal ways of knowing.

It may seem that teachers have little time in school for the contemplation needed to nourish their creativity and intuitive skills. It would be simple to set aside just a few moments of time between classes that are specifically devoted to re-energizing. This would help faculty regroup and re-charge before the next group of students arrive in the classroom. Music, sound, and harmonics can be used to enhance this process. If sound and movement were an active part of learning during class time, students might be less aggressive in the hallways, which are currently the only time allotted for secondary students to be mobile within the school day, with the exception of lunch period and physical education.

As students and staff gain confidence in their perceptual skills, they can listen more objectively to others and develop more gentle approaches within themselves. In these moments, we experience our graciousness, and offer the same to those we encounter. This requires space enough to pause throughout the day, and literally sense the deeper aspects of "*who*" we are in the moment.

Creating Beauty – and Transformation -- in Schools

For hundreds of thousands of years, people have been drawn to the outdoors seeking the solace, inspiration, and wonder experienced in nature. The colors and tones of nature are relaxing to the eyes, ears, mind – the entire body. The elements of nature -- air, wind, fire, water, and space -- work in balance with one another and we experience this balance when we sit under a shady tree, or near a babbling brook. Our body is even comprised of the elements, which keep us in balance. Nature feeds our body with energy, joy, and inspiration.

All of the best elements of nature – greenery, sounds, smells -- can be brought into lessons in schools and their surrounding communities. Why would we want to do this, you're asking? It is through our balance with nature that a much-needed shift in emotional awareness can take place. Youth who are in touch with their bodies are more sensitive to the light, sound, and external stimuli created through technological advances. They sense these stimuli; they process them and seek balance in their day-to-day experiences. This may seem obvious, but we all know children who are simply not aware of their surroundings. They are missing out on much of life! I am in full support of public education creating opportunities for children to discover their innate beauty, no holds barred.

Bringing nature into the classroom is actually a fairly easy task. Fabrics, paint colors, lighting, paintings and art, small animals such as fish, and aromatherapy can be used to enhance schools and create a learning environment that is comfortable and emotionally appealing for the learner. Rocks, plants, crystals, shells, and other forms of plant and mineral life also give students a sense of the elements that they are naturally in tune with. Time and time again students and staff comment on how "peaceful, nice, soothing, and lovely" my classroom feels. My students and I both enjoyed learning in a classroom that was aesthetically pleasing, but more than that, creating beauty in the classroom and school building gives students an opportunity to enhance and take ownership of their learning environment. Using nature reminds students that they are part something larger and encourages balance in their lives.

How Whole Can We Go? The Gaia Hypothesis

I noticed a statue of Gaia on the counter of a shop while I was discussing our educational system with the storeowner. Gaia or Gaea is the name given to the primordial planetary goddess by the ancient Greeks who has been worshiped since the stone-age. In contemporary times, Gaia is known as Mother Earth or Mother Nature. Her names are plentiful, crossing many cultures, some of which include: Prithvi (Hindu), Iya Aye (Yoruba), Kuna Pippi (Australia) and Pachamama (Peru).

The artist of this sculpture, Oberon Zell, placed a very clear intention on creating it. It was made immediately following a mystical experience, which altered the course of his life. Zell was compelled to create a sculpture that would honor the evolution of Gaia and the importance of teaching people to care for our planet and keep her from harm's way.

I held the statue, and as I admired her, I felt a pulsing electrical current run through my hands into my arms and up and down my torso until the crown of my head or (chakra-energy center) opened. I immediately thought of my research project. I took that as a cue that it was important that I address our planet in a more direct manner than I had planned, linking the Gaia Hypothesis, or Gaia Theory (which basically states that the earth – despite its many different physical systems – operates as one single system).

This learning experience triggered my imagination and touched my heart. I wondered about the most important things our children could learn. I thought about our planet and how much we take for granted. I thought about the devastating effects that over-consumption and over-population have created for our environment. I felt the misuse of power that stripped the dignity from our indigenous people, "the guardians of the planet," and how much we could learn from our native brothers and sisters. I imagined how powerful it would be to bring lessons to our schools that teach personal well-being and the well-being of the family, community, country, and planet. Using the Gaia hypothesis, wouldn't this be a better world if we learned to share our resources and take care of one another? What would our lives be like, if we experienced ourselves as part of one human family and our mother earth?

9 (photo of Gaia statue purchased in Schenectady, New York July 2004)

Native American Tribal Elder Frank Walthers explains, "to Indians, the Earth is not inanimate. It is a living entity, the mother of all life, our Mother Earth. All her children, everything in nature is alive: the living stone, the great breathing mountains, trees, and plants, as well as birds and animals and man. All are united in one harmonious whole" (quoted in Zell 3).

We are connected to all life. When we acknowledge our connection with appreciation and reverence, we experience nature on a sensate level. It is through this connection that we understand who we are, deeply and wholly. Through our connection to nature, we maintain balance and center. This ideology is also held as sacred among our indigenous people, who view the self, community, world, and cosmos as one unified, interconnected entity. "I am you and you are me, I see" and "We might survive as brothers here or perish here as fools" reminds us that all humanity is part of a unified whole responsible to our planet. Educators, administrators, and our political leaders have a responsibility to guide our students to "walk softly" on our planet honoring her wisdom through nature. When all life is honored, we can create communities that are self-sustaining. Our future depends on it.

Students deserve the opportunity to understand the relevancy of what they are learning in relationship to the world that they live in, to see the "big picture," so to speak, that everything is part of one. Students need exposure to different environments for this to occur. This also ties into my idea of bringing nature into the learning environment. Nature offers bountiful opportunities for communion, relaxation, scientific discovery, and relevancy to children of all ages, and their instructors.

Spiritual Intelligence, Emotional Intelligence and Holistic Education

Some may argue that the educational system is not the appropriate venue to introduce Emotional Intelligence or Consciousness. Joe Bruchac and the late Marcia Dale Lopez address the issue of standardized evaluation of the learning experience in the film: "European education is widely didactic [...]" and "[there is something much more to learning than being able to regurgitate concepts that somebody had told you [...]. Holistic education reflects and responds more fully than conventional education to the changing needs of our youth, because it supports personal transformation."

Scott H. Forbes shared the view of many holistic educators as far back as his speech at the Third Annual Conference on Education, Spirituality, and the Whole Child back in June of 1996. Forbes noted that as humanity changes its "view of itself," schools must change their teaching methods, or risk having an educational system that is felt to be meaningless by the very population it wants to serve (Miller 14). Consider the following:

1. For youth to become knowledgeable, they must be ready and motivated to learn and capable of integrating new information into their lives.

2. For youth to become responsible, they must be able to understand risks and opportunities and be motivated to choose actions and behaviors that serve their own interests and the interests of others.

3. For youth to be caring they must be able to see beyond themselves and appreciate concerns for others; they must believe that to care is to be part of a community that is welcoming, nurturing, and concerned about them (McCarthy 1).

In my experience, students need opportunities to actively engage in the learning process in the school, community, and nature. Systems reflect the level of consciousness of society. Individual teachers who provide creative learning experiences in our schools feel the strain of creating in isolation. School systems built upon the principles of holistic education can support the process of transformative learning. We've witnessed the positive outcomes available in highly functioning public charter schools and private schools that embody holistic principles or integrative teaching models.

We can understand emotional intelligence as a connection between heart and mind. Although most research indicates that individuals develop Emotional Intelligence during the first 16 years of life, with clear intention, we can continue to increase their Emotional Intelligence throughout our lives.

Here's an example of a holistic, transformative lesson offered to students at Schenectady High School: *Sixty students researched topics they selected dealing with children in crisis. Those who interviewed specialists in their field of study as part of their research noted a change in their own perspective and a sense of compassion for the individuals involved in their research. In other words, their eyes were opened to see a more complete picture of the children they were studying, including the environments these children came from and how they were affected by their surroundings. Most students said hearing personal stories from adults with first-hand experience in their research topics made the learning process "interesting and more real."* Giving students the opportunity to present their research in a format that was meaningful to them made their learning experience more interesting, engaging, and relevant. Students wrote poetry, and songs created infomercials, hosted educational talk shows and game shows, and shared their research with peers in small assemblies. Finding ways to create community in school is vital for students who do not come from stable home environments. I witnessed a profound level of compassion, understanding, and support for learning from the students in the class, especially when they shared their research projects with their peers. All but one student felt that this form of evaluation was life changing.

Transformation becomes natural as we open and become receptive to the process of exploring with curiosity. Transformative learning is cyclical, it shifts and expands. This process is continual and progressive. Schools can be designed to inspire our young people in the natural process of learning from the inside out, and in discovering their passions aspiring to reach their potential. Teachers have just as much to gain from these experiences.

In the film Dreaming New Schools, Joe Bruchac explains that Native American cultures offer holistic learning experiences that connect learning with nature.

Holistic Learning and Cultural Sensitivity

Becoming culturally responsive can help reduce the incidence of student "turn off" because of socio-cultural differences, like process-oriented learning (where the action involved in discovery and learning is valued as much as or more than the end result) and product-oriented learning (where grading student's achievement is used as a comprehensive analysis of student achievement). Cultures that practice process-oriented learning rather than product-oriented learning may have difficulty in the conceptualization and execution of learning. If the term *cultural* is broadened to include diversity of learning styles, the opportunity for learning on many levels is profoundly increased.

Joe Wittmer, author of **Valuing Similarity and Diversity,** uses an extremely creative approach in addressing the need for educators and scholars to develop culturally sensitive interpersonal skills. Wittmer asks educators and scholars from many cultural backgrounds to share their insights concerning communication styles within their own culture of origin. He applies their viewpoints to teaching strategies that promote sensitivity and awareness in the classroom. This creates a safe learning environment where students are respected for valuing their cultural identity and appreciating the other cultures. It also reduces the risk of un-intentionally teaching from a cultural bias. Most importantly, it creates an environment of one-ness, where no one is "alien," although we may all be different from one another.

Gregory Cajete, Ph.D., has written several texts on Native American epistemology relevant to educators teaching indigenous children. In his most recent text, *Igniting the Sparkle,* Cajete includes teaching models that can be applied to all indigenous cultures. He explains that in Western science, information is classified through conceptual reasoning, which is geared towards students who are analytical, objective, structured, and verbal. This is fine for students who are inclined to learn that way, but many students are not. There are differences in learning styles that reflect left-brain and right-brain synthesis as well as socio-cultural differences, and Cajete observes, "many Native Americans tend to be intuitive, subjective, non-verbal, synthesizing, and oriented to wholes with practical application to their learning" (Cajete 15). As the Western scientific model continues to move from theories of reductionism towards whole systems of living, teaching models such as Cajete's can be adapted to the larger academic community where *all* children can honor cultural diversity and promote wholeness: personally, communally, and globally.

Holism and Listening

Our educational institutions shape the moral development of our youth. This requires integrity and ethics in learning positive interpersonal skills like communication. John Beaulieu, Ph.D. describes speaking as "the movement of sacred sound-seeking expression" (Beaulieu 54), Cultivating a reverence for life through compassionate speech and listening skills has not been a focus in educational training.

Schools are desperately seeking ways to resolve conflicts among students and build stronger, united learning communities. Character Education programs like "Peer Mediation" and "Character Counts" train faculty to work with students in solving conflicts. Recent studies show that programs supporting non-violent communication, social and emotional learning, and peaceful practices fostered at young ages and continued through the middle and secondary years are most effective. Students come to see and understand the benefit of safely expressing their feelings and needs and practicing non-violent behavior. There is an opportunity to promote nonviolence in all schools through school pedagogy, philosophies, mission statements and curriculum.

In 2004, I attended Dr. Jean Houston's 10-day leadership seminar in Social Artistry. Carol Hwoschinsky led a session on deep listening skills, which I found extremely insightful. Hwoschinsky based her work on Arthur Kessler's Hierarchy for Compassionate Listening. Dr. Houston works collaboratively with the UNDP (United Nations Developmental Program) in countries that are struggling with deep seeded conflict considered at risk such as Israel and Palestine.

Participants in the seminar completed several exercises designed create an extremely safe space to explore deep listening skills. The guidelines of these techniques support the intuitive process and personal transformation as seen in the CPPT and how they can be applied to relationship skills. Their use implies that authentic communication can contribute to growth and transformation. I found this exercise to be an extraordinarily liberating experience where speaking from the heart was honored, respected, and heard.

Hwoschinsky's guidelines for the practice of compassionate listening include:

(1) Being silent, reviewing the guidelines and set a clear intention
(2) Not trying to "fix" the problem
(3) Having compassion for the speaker's situation
(4) Listening from your heart
(5) Reflecting back to the speaker
(6) Avoiding asking "why" and
(7) Allowing silence during the process.

Tips for the speaker include speaking from the heart, listening to the body and sensing when you do not feel compassionate.

Clarity of intention and determining appropriate curriculum to incorporate compassionate listening skills would be something to consider when using this process in an academic setting. I witnessed the powerful skill of deeply listening first-hand. Students know when they are being fully seen, and acknowledged, rather than spoken at, and I can honestly say that since this seminar, my teaching skills have never been the same. Incorporating compassionate listening skills into curriculum provides an opportunity for students and staff to establish personal dialogue with meaning and purpose. This in turn increases students' sense of dignity, respect, and self-esteem. As they pass these skills on in their own communication, opportunity for an environment of acceptance and one-ness becomes possible.

Teaching Peace as a Compassionate Practice

Leading students and staff in non-violent communication – with the end result being a sense of wholeness as a community -- is one possibility that would be quite manageable in public school settings.

In 2013, I was introduced to the theory of nonviolent communication, (NVC). My limited exposure to this process became transformative. In practicing NVC, I learned to identify my feelings more clearly and to help identify the unmet need of others. As I practiced in class, I became more compassionate and gained clarity. Because our needs were being expressed, we were safe to explore issues more deeply, without fearing the judgment that can separate us.

I have learned that educators teach peace through *embodying* peace. This is not to say that we are capable of being peaceful every moment of the day but cultivating the skill to choose a peaceful attitude can become a practice. Being peaceful is a natural process as we develop a keen awareness of our subtle energy body, the body intuitively responds harmoniously. Peace becomes a kinesthetic experience. The harmonious wave frequencies will permeate the classroom over a period of time, much like the peacefulness one experiences in a temple, or high on a mountain. I loved hearing students comment on "how chill" our classroom "felt," especially when the overall temperament of the building was in turmoil.

Higher academic institutes such as The University of Hawaii recognize the need for resolving conflict on a global scale by offering cutting-edge training in resolving conflicts through peaceful measures. Back in 1986, the Board of Regents of the University of Hawaii recognized the urgent and universal desire for peace and oneness in the world. The final outcome of this investigation was the establishment of the Spark M. Matsunga Institute for Peace. Their program on Conflict Resolution aims to engage in research that furthers an understanding of disputes and dispute settlement practices and encourages the practice and testing of a variety of dispute resolution procedures. It is known for its emphasis and expertise in the cross-cultural aspects of conflict.

As more universities introduce educational programs that include whole systems of learning, the secondary education system may follow course. Developing holistic, multi-cultural instructional programs including our multiple intelligences can prepare our youth to become responsible, responsive global citizens. This process will create opportunities for transformative learning as well. The choice is ours, as expressed in the musical interlude from One Giant Leap, "We might survive as brothers here or perish here as fools."

Chapter Six

"We delight in the beauty of the butterfly, but rarely admit the changes it has gone through to achieve that beauty."
Maya Angelou

Principle Five: Small Learning Communities Support Transformative Learning

Principle five may very well be the most challenging hurdle for authentic re-design of public education, because it addresses our current paradigm straight on. We must choose to learn about learning to help students reach their potential as innately creative, intelligent beings. The Magic happens in the classroom, and beyond in spite of the large arena surrounding the highly effective teacher and his/her students, one might even say, against all odds.

11 Students from SHS participate in Mental Health Conference at the NYS Capital in Albany, NY Spring 2010

Small (er) Learning Communities

To prove the point that less is sometimes more, I will keep this chapter short and sweet. What I'm really talking about in this chapter is creating a learning environment that fully supports a deep sense of quality in the way teachers can relate with their students, through connection.

Public, Private or Charter Schools, what's your viewpoint?

- Do you believe that students who attend public schools should have the same opportunities as children who attend private schools?
- Why do many of our leaders in public policy, and government officials attend private schools?
- Do we want all students to reach their potential?
- Do we see all children's gifts as equal in value?
- How do we qualify skills and talents?
- How can public schools emulate the nurturing qualities found in smaller, private schools? And lastly,
- How can public schools provide equal opportunity for all students?

How Size, Design, and Intention Impact Transformative Learning

All living beings need attention to thrive. Humanity is no exception. A school is only as strong as the leaders who steward the school. There are many schools that are taking initiatives in addressing this issue, by creating *authentic* small learning communities comprised of like-minded, dedicated staff, and administration whose goal is to put the needs of the children above all else. These schools can be used as models for the impending systemic change at hand.

Many schools, however, have leaders that are not in sync with each other. Combine this with large populations of students who have not witnessed or personally experienced positive change or who don't believe that they have great potential to become agents of change, and you wind up with a group of kids who believe they're going nowhere in life. The size and structure of large schools is challenged offering quality education, especially in underserved communities.

Paradigms influence the decision-making policies towards an established institution, like public education. Willingness to explore these assumptions is a courageously bold step because it takes us beyond our comfort zone, and challenges present habits, beliefs, assumptions, and ultimately behaviors towards one another.

I'd like to explore the core qualities of leadership, resilience, and sustainability often available in smaller schools, whether private or public, which become extremely difficult to sustain in large school districts. These qualities can be distilled to four main areas: 1) mindfulness 2) collaborative decision making 3) transparency in communication and disseminating information and 4) receptivity or being open to new ideas. These qualities are essential for educational organizations to run smoothly and effectively.

Self-aware, compassionate, strong, humble leaders are needed to endure the challenges faced in our national school crisis. Administrators, and educators trust one another when they embody ethics, as a core value system. MBSR and other secular contemplative practices can be an essential part of teacher training and administrative training as well. Legislation and State Departments of Education play a major role in evolving educational policies to meet the needs of the twenty first century. Administrators and staff can explore more democratic school policies, including the role of the government in education. I have witnessed first-hand, that when trust breaks down, true collaboration is impossible. Without collaboration, there is little room for learning.

Like many teachers in inner-city schools, I am well aware that the structure in which we are working is frail at its core and held together by the great *fear* of change, as well as the resistance that change often brings about. Large groups who feel threatened by new ideas often feed off of one another, creating chaos, depression, and more disparity. It is very difficult to change a collective viewpoint that models "this is the best we can do, under the circumstances." Many teachers feel powerless to make changes and believe that they *cannot* changes because administrators make administrative decisions. Administrators make administrative evaluations. This makes it nearly impossible to "clean up and clear out" those who do not have our children's interests at heart. Imagine the possibilities when learning communities are in collective agreement to a higher consciousness!

This is why I suggest that the campaign for small learning communities be seriously considered by those who are in authority to make the systemic changes possible. I also believe that teachers can remember that *they* – more than anyone else in society -- have the potential to influence and impact lives on a personal level. They cannot allow outside agents to undermine their responsibility, which is to serve the students. Teachers in large schools with large groups of individuals who feel despondent need extra support. This includes "down time" to rejuvenate and gain clarity.

Smaller Class Settings Can Make a Difference

Research has shown that small learning communities work best when the learning community is no larger than two hundred students (Meier). However, many school districts have consolidated in order to save on the ever-increasing costs of education. It is not uncommon for a High School in New York State to have more than two thousand students in the building at one time (Meier).

When students see themselves as a community of learners who impact one another and behave responsibly towards each other. I've seen relationships flourish and students show concern and compassion for one another countless times. We've shared stories, laughter, and kindness. I am grateful for the many lessons I have learned through my experiences with my students.

This doesn't mean that all hope is lost in large school districts. They need support in finding the financial means to build additional facilities so that students and staff experience a true small learning community or downsize to support students' learning process. Larger school districts creating schools within a school still face the problem of students still swimming in a large fishbowl. Ultimately, smaller class sizes and increased support staff can be available for students. Common planning time supports staff in developing interdisciplinary curriculum, troubleshooting, and supporting students with special needs. Small learning communities give students the opportunity to make personal connections with the adult staff in the building.

Small Learning Communities are an Economically Sound Choice

If we want students to contribute to the advancement of society, then let's do it well. We want our next generation to become self-confident, creatively intelligent explorers who take risks, practice empathy and are able to take other's viewpoints into consideration. This takes quality time, effort, and design to accomplish. Designing buildings and schedules that foster nurturing learning environments is not for the weary hearted, and extremely important at this time in our development.

Highly populated school districts are subject to the financial constraints of housing thousands of students within a school building. Standardization becomes a necessity due to the sheer size of the school. Schools have become large financial institutions constantly bartering for grants and other incentives that bring in a cash flow. This system is not conducive to transformative learning. Smaller schools and classes accompanied by trained paraprofessional support holistic lessons. Involving faculty in the decision-making process will help them feel more vested in the program.

The "top down" approach to leadership in this case is a major hurdle, which can be evaluated and upgraded. Impeccability becomes the standard set by faculty and administration. All personnel are viewed as equal in importance of this system to function as a unified whole. Authentic leadership supporting the good of a whole, unified system enhances all its participants. Leadership of the twenty-first century demands no less than this level of integrity.

Teachers and administrators trained in Mindfulness and Social and Emotional Learning, provide rich learning experiences. Together, we can create safe learning environments for all students and staff to explore.

Structural Design and its Impact on Learning; A Renaissance in Public Education

Daniel Pink NY Times Best Seller, A Whole New Mind brilliantly describes the important role that design (is now playing and will continue to play in the next century, something I intuitively sensed about my classroom. Taking design in structure of future schools offers an opportunity for beauty, sensibility, environmentally sustainable atmospheres where learning is supported on many levels.

A disconnect from our natural environment disconnects us from one another. Using soothing calming and exciting sensory experiences in the design of schools (or whatever we call them) in the future can only has a positive impact on learning, living, and overall well-being.

We are Growing in Conscious Awareness

In the sixties and seventies, a very large yellow bird reminded us that "kids are people too", on a television series called Sesame Street. I often wonder what we thought they were before the song rang loud and clear, reaching the masses on public television. I couldn't help but notice that children and young people carry a level of sophistication and interest in psycho-spiritual development that was not a part of our collective consciousness fifty years ago. Their interests range from introspection, energy dynamics and healing connection with the elements, psychic abilities, to indigenous cultures, historic icons, and extra-terrestrial affairs, across age groups and cultures and socioeconomic backgrounds. Their understanding of equality and social justice and need for inclusion in the creative process are evident. Relating to our youth and becoming aware of their interests and needs is a vital step to take.

Transparency, Ethics, and Taking Responsibility for our Actions

To me, transparency is courageous work. Transparency is about healing. It is not a punishment, or a rule for judgment, or finding out about things we may have done that we now regret, and experience as shame. Transparency is the doorway to understanding that we are growing as a society, and are interested in learning from our mistakes, without judgment.

The Heart of the Matter

I am an educator who is devoted to lifelong learning because I believe with all my heart and soul that every child has unique, untapped potential, waiting to be explored. And I believe that this exploration is the promise of our future. Creative, wholesome, nurturing environments support that process. ***But more importantly, our judgments, beliefs and attitudes towards equality, potential, justice, learning, creativity, and everything you can imagine shape our relatedness to these children that we hold so dear. Our future depends on gaining clarity and healing these judgments, beliefs, and attitudes.***

Teaching Cooperation

Teaching cooperation is a skill that requires modeling cooperation for its value to be understood and learned. In large institutions that have followed a regimented form of behavior based on a chain of command, being open to new concept, ideas, and ways of relating poses some interesting challenges in terms of developing cooperative skills. When a system become rigid in its orientation of following procedures, the human element of cooperation is left aside, and all rational thought process seem to go out the window.

Parents and teachers probably understand the value of teaching a child the skill of cooperation better than anyone else. In early childhood education cooperation is actually considered a developmental task. The developmental stage that proceeds cooperative play is called "parallel play", where two children could be seen playing side by side, each engrossed in their own experience of play with little or no interaction between one another. The two-year-old does not have the brain/social emotional development to understand the concept of cooperation. Cooperative play can be demonstrated through play at around the age of three, when the child has the capacity to see, feel the world from a less egocentric stance, which can be shown by sharing the toy, or participating in a game like "make believe". This skill, like all human growth, especially in the social/emotional realm is not a linear process. In one moment, we may see the child sharing their toy, and in the next minute the child has a need to feel their relationship to the toy by claiming ownership, ("It's mine").

Take a large institution like education for example where organizational design is pretty complicated. Policy makers determine the "rules of the game", with a set of objectives (or standards) that are determined to be the unit of measure for success or failure (winning or losing the game". The policy makers, however, are not on the same team as the institution they are directing policy towards, so there is no physical contact or opportunity to share ideas and get feedback from individual schools that are affected

Here are some ideas for practicing servant leadership.

IN PRACTICE

1. *Recognize how our actions impact others.*

2. *Model positive communication, and practice care and consideration.*

3. *Take an interest in what others are experiencing around you and learn about their challenges, and victories.*

4. *Take time out to meet with those who play an integral part in your work environment.*

5. *Practice flexibility, and willingness to get input from the outside frequently.*

by the policies set forth in "real time". There is a breakdown or disconnect in the organization that is not systemic at its core but is being presented as though it was indeed a system.

The school leaders follow the state mandates with little wiggle room for creative measure to address the personal needs of their unique learning community and proceed to give the rules to the teachers who are expected to diligently follow them. Teachers then in turn tell the rules to the students. Rules, standards, and policy become the benchmark for determining growth, development, and even success. We've all witnessed the gruesome outcome of the design in place, and the outcome of common practice of the adage "do as I say, not as I do")

6. *Practice self- reflection and be brutally honest with yourself about how cooperative you actually are.*

7. *Build bridges in your community through authentic communication.*

8. *Know the rules but understand the value of flexibility within the system of rules in place.*

Cooperation requires creativity, coupled with and a level of social and emotional maturity, expressed as a willingness to practice empathy, by hearing, and understanding another's point of view. It might even require a level of humility in acknowledging that another may have an idea that might work "better" than the ideas of those who control the system that is in place. The problem with "top down" management is that no one likes how it feels to be controlled, and authentic inclusion in the decision-making process invites opportunity for change and growth that is immeasurable. The need to be valued and take responsibility can become a cooperative effort.

Cooperation can be practiced on an interpersonal level, which can ultimately have a sustaining impact on the larger systems in place, after all people created these systems in the first place.

Cooperation is a precursor to collaboration, and a skill that must be mastered to effect the change that is sorely needed in public education. Open communication between policy makers, school leaders, and the adults working with students, and yes, even students themselves is the crossroad to this process.

I'm not an expert in systems change, but I dedicated my career to helping young people develop and value cooperative skills that they can apply to their daily lives. *Can the adults who are at the forefront of decisions that impact our society agree to cooperate?* I hope so!

Chapter Seven

"Music [...] gives soul to the universe, wings to the mind, flight to the imagination, and charm and gaiety to life and to everything."
Plato

Scientific Research, Sound, and Healing; What's the Relationship?

"Sound is Sacred. In all religious and spiritual traditions sound, word and music are instrumental in creating and sustaining the universe, nature, and humankind. Healing sounds are a part of a 'sacred therapy' still practiced among holy men and women, shamans and healers, and indigenous peoples of the earth."

(Pat Moffitt Cooke Introduction)

Teaching at Schenectady, with over forty nations represented sparked my interest in the "soundscape" of different cultures. As I became more interested in how we relate to ourselves, and others, I began to explore profound the impact that sound can have on our state of being collectively and individually. In the following section, I share some of what I have learned through my doctoral research.

Wellness and healing are one aspect of personal transformation supported by the Creative Process of Personal Transformation, and relate to my doctoral research question, "How can multicultural sound be used in a learning community?" The narratives in this section were designed to give examples and personal accounts of where sound and harmonics were used for healing and self-awareness. They discuss discoveries concerning the power of harmonics and the role that intention plays in creative processes using sound.

Keep in mind, that sound, rhythm, healing, and personal transformation are passions of mine. In the following section, I share the discoveries I made when I dove into the study of healing sounds and

Imagine the levels of knowing students might encounter if teachers mindfully guided students through direct experience in areas they wish to explore. Can we imagine students experiencing "mindful" math lessons, "mindful" science lessons, and "mindful" music?

rhythms. These discoveries were made during my internship in India and Peru, and with musicians and artists from various cultures here in the US.

Keeping The Day in Balance

The rhythm of energy flow has a profound impact on group dynamics. Recognizing these patterns of flow, can impact how we respond. I've discovered that being mindful of tone, energy flow, and behaviors and having a keen sense of emotional intelligence has a profound impact on the classroom climate. And this is really a form of using our creative intelligence of plugging into that energy that I have as a Multi-Dimensional Creative Being. This skill can be applied across content areas. Learning to listen to the rhythm and the cues of the body, accessing our feelings and trusting our instincts is an important aspect of the intuitive process.

Taking time to tune into the energy flow of the classroom and each student is a *respectful* choice. We enter the classroom with an anticipated lesson to explore with our students. As the facilitator of the group, we are open to the needs of the group *and* individual students if we are to achieve optimum growth. This is anything but an easy task. Secondary school schedules move students through the school building every forty to fifty-five minutes. The day is fragmented in subject matter as well since little interdisciplinary work is integrated across curricula. Most teachers are not aware of subject matter that is being taught in other subjects during the course of any given day. As curriculum becomes more interdisciplinary, learning is more relevant and integrated, and students find meaning and purpose to what they are learning. Curriculum development is just one way we can support our interconnectedness and explore unity within diversity.

Students, teachers, and administrators have busy, often hectic days. Centering by taking a deep breath until we feel a balanced energy flow in our body increases self-awareness. Centered, educators offers opportunity for students to experience or sense what balance feels like. Since our natural state of awareness is balanced and whole, the body will naturally entrain itself towards balance if the learning environment is safe and inclusive. This takes practice. And I consider this skill an ongoing process. Each teacher has their own unique teaching style, and will have their own style of managing, assessing, and engaging energetically with their students. However, students are most comfortable when teachers are authentic, so it will be important to use a *"grounding"* or balancing medium that you're comfortable with.

It is great for students and staff to experience different techniques. Encouraging curiosity offers many opportunities to explore. Contemplative practices like mindfulness, provide opportunity to experience self from a more expanded view.

For example, I've practiced exercises with my students to help them sense their own energy flow, and to help reduce tension, re-invigorate, or focus their attention. If their energy is dragging in the classroom, we might pause the lesson for a few moments and stand and breathe deeply or move our arms above our heads. Sometimes we do yoga postures or deep breathing to relax or increase energy flow. In 2010 I was introduced to Mindfulness-Based Stress Reduction and recognize the usefulness of its practice. I like to ask the students to notice how their bodies feel before and after the exercises, because these practices have a cumulative effect on the body, since entrainment is a natural progression in terms of body awareness.

Music and Rhythmic Activities

Music and rhythm are exceptional mediums that support flow and can positively impact moods. I like using Donna Eden's work "Energy Medicine" in the classroom too. It is quite practical, and students are surprised at the quick turn-around they experience in reducing stress and stabilizing their energy. I have found that my students related particularly well to Eden's cross-crawl exercise, because it reminds them of athletic warmups. I use terms that they can relate to, and I have discovered that science provides wonderful language supporting holism.

In our fast-paced technological society, individuals may feel pressured to spend the day accomplishing increasingly more tasks with little regard for the warning signals the body sends when it is out of harmony.

The "Our Natural Rhythms" section was designed as a reminder of the importance of finding balance in our lives by becoming more in tune with nature's rhythms.

Can you imagine the positive impact taking the time daily to become familiar with our own body's rhythm, or its energy flow would have? My own personal practice included daily meditation and quick breaks between periods (often in the restroom, where I wouldn't be interrupted for a few minutes). I would breathe from head to toe releasing any imbalances in my body before my next class. There was a noticeable difference in my disposition when I took the time to balance.

I'd like to refer back to my statement concerning the "anticipated" lesson of the day. It's very important to be prepared with the lesson for the day, but equally important to become comfortable allowing flexibility and openness to experiences in the classroom generated by students. (We could also say that this is tuning into the rhythm of the class!) Some of our most interesting lessons happen when we as a class allow the present moment to guide us. The *"Milagro pequeno,"* or teachable moment, often arises when we least expect it!

I'm also interested in harmonics in terms of how they are integrated in nature. I discovered that our biological systems carry a harmonic frequency, which is palpable when we pay close attention to the sensory mechanisms produced by our body. For example, our heart and blood beat and flow in rhythm when we are in good health. Our respiration has a rhythm that is unique to each person. Our bones carry the resonance of sounds that we hear each moment we are awake or asleep. We flow in and out of sync with our own harmonic flow of energy and rhythm, depending on the activities that we participate in daily.

Steven Halpern describes sound and harmonic frequencies (or *integrals*) as "a carrier of wave consciousness" (www.healingsounds.com). This indicates that our intention has much to do with the experience of using harmonics or other healing modalities for personal transformation. Declaring a clear intent for healing and transformation is an important aspect of this process. I view healing and transformation as a process, which facilitates the body being in harmony with itself and functioning as a balanced whole. When our body and mind are balanced, we feel better and experience greater harmony and joy. Balance is intrinsic to personal growth.

Music and Crossing Cultural Borders

Different languages carry specific harmonic frequencies that we may not be familiar with, resulting in a form of culture shock. In some of his earlier research, Dr. Alfred Tomatis discovered that each language predominantly uses a different set of frequencies. For example, the French language uses mainly frequencies between 1,000 and 2,000 Hz. French ears are thus accustomed to these frequencies. British people are accustomed to listen to frequencies between 2,000 and 12,000 Hz, so they are "deaf" to the French sounds (and *vice-versa*). Tomatis found that you can train the ear to get accustomed to the foreign frequencies to learn foreign languages more easily. In broader terms, this means that *in order to fully learn, you have to listen!*

Each culture weaves its mythology and stories into their music. We can sense each culture's story through the sounds, rhythms, tones, pitch, and scales used. The music paints a picture of the way that the culture interacts with its participants. Stop for a moment and recall the last time you listened to music from another culture. What kind of music was it, and what feelings did it evoke? Did you feel in tune or resonate with its harmonic frequencies?

Could it be that as we expose ourselves to new cultures and actively listen with open hearts and minds, we may become more attuned to the harmonic systems of other cultures? What are the implications of this process? Might we be more accepting of the world around us? Or might we even learn quite a bit about ourselves?

Harmonics and Personal Healing

Jonathan Goldman, pioneer in sound healing and cross-cultural contemplative practices, has developed two theories supporting the use of harmonics for personal growth and healing, based on the principles of hermetic harmonics. According to Goldman, the universe is an endless number of vibrating rhythms that we can tap into to achieve balance and become more enlightened.

His two formulas are:

- Frequency +Intention= Healing (or harmonically pure frequency sung with clear intention are healing energies)
- Visualization + Vocalization = Manifestation (or clearly visualizing through thought and vocalizing, the same thought creates a resonant field for manifestation)

These formulas suggest that combining vocalizing and visualization creates a resident field (a ripe environment, in other words) for manifestation. The intention to use sound for healing purposes in this case is based on the premise that sound waves have a direct impact on the energy body. (This concept is intrinsic to Eastern practices and linked to Principle One of the Five Principles of Transformative Learning.)

Masaru Emoto's controversial work supports Goldman's theory demonstrating the power of intention in a pseudo-clinical setting. Emoto collected thousands of water samples from many parts of the world using frozen crystallized water samples as a medium to demonstrate the power of thought. Using identical water samples, Emoto instructed a group of people to direct thoughts towards collected samples of water and then froze the water to determine crystallization formations. Although Emoto has not conducted a controlled study, his work has gained international momentum. This indicates an interest in self-awareness and healing on a global scale. I, for one would be very interested in continued research in this area.

Harmonic systems intrinsic to ancient wisdom teachings of Eastern cultures such as Hinduism may be expressed by the term *nada brahma,* or *the world is sound.* Using harmonics and music as healing modalities surfaced in the U.S. in the twentieth century when Willem Vad de Wall established the first institutional music program at Pennsylvania's Allentown State Hospital (Goldman). Pioneers such as Jonathan Goldman, Kay Gardner, Jorge Alfano, Mitchell Gaynor, Pat Moffitt Cooke, John Beaulieu, and Paul Newham are exploring healing modalities, using the laws of intervals and harmonics. These practitioners and scholars concur that it is extremely important to maintain integrity with clear intention while using harmonics for healing, expanding states of consciousness, and creating balance in the body.

Clinical & Field Research in Harmonics and Sound as Energy

One of the first contemporary scientists to do research in the area of harmonic frequencies was Dr. Alfred Tomatis, well known for his research in APP (Audio Psycho Phonology), in the early 1950's. APP addresses the capacity for increasing our listening skills by training the two bones in our inner ear through exposure to harmonic frequencies absent from the normal listening range (Lawton). These missing frequencies may occur from isolated exposure to cultural harmonic systems, trauma, and extra-ordinary sensory activity such as autism and ADD.

Tomatis maintains that the bones carry a harmonic resonant field in our body, and this resonant field creates a muffled auditory experience. Because the bones are not gated like the ear, they allow sensations in the body without discrimination (Lawton). Tomatis desensitized the bone conduction by sending gated musical frequencies directly to the bone to increase listening capacity. In essence, he trained people to listen with their bodies.

Swiss scientist Dr. Hans Jenny followed Tomatis' research developing the harmonic theory called Cymatics in the early 1990's (Thompson). Cymatics applies harmonics to thousands of inorganic structures (liquids, pastes, and the like) by placing them on steel plates and then vibrating the plates with different frequencies. He discovered that each frequency produced a distinct shape, demonstrating that sound waves have the capacity to affect matter.

Most people recognize the power of sound and the effect that it has on our emotions (imagine watching a film without music); however, Jenny's work has powerful implications for the use of sound in healing modalities. At the end of his research, Jenny concluded that it was necessary to continue doing research in Cymatics involving the voice, speech, and the larynx

You can see examples of listening with our bodies in the "African American Tale", the "Natural Rhythms" section, playing Middle Eastern Drum with Layne Redmond and "Modah Ani" during the film credits.

(Thompson). The following picture demonstrates Dr. Jenny's research noting the effect of harmonic frequencies in inorganic material.

The vowel A in sand

Pic 12 (www.neuroacoustics.com)

Toning to Release Negative Energy

Laurel Elizabeth Keys is a nun who began using *toning* as part of her meditative practice. Keys discovered toning in the 1960's. Toning can best be described as "something available to anyone who goes through the mechanics of letting the voice express itself in a natural way" (Keys 6). It is a "positive, consciously directed identification with the inner power of life, and the full awareness of releasing it at will" (Keys 10).

According to Keys, toning is an intuitive process, which involves looking inward and simply feeling. Sensing the body, the client is instructed first to groan freely without reservation. Groaning, Keys explains, allows all of the hurts and suffering that we have experienced to surface, therefore releasing repressed feelings from the body. The client observes the sensations without judgment and continues groaning until the body releases a sigh of relief.

Keys, directs the client to replace these emotions with feelings of purpose. Keys stresses the importance of intention in the process of toning, stating that "without the person's own effort to recognize the cause and remove it, they became dependent upon the toning" (Keys 45) rather than healing the emotional wound. She maintains that hundreds of individuals have been healed by some natural force, not yet recognized, something also experienced through toning. She does not have control experiments to support her testimony, only the gratitude of the many individuals she has worked with. Some cases include a skin cancer patient with no re-occurrences for six years, a diabetic who recovered her vision, and Keys' own self-healing. She does not claim that toning is one hundred percent effective, nor does she claim to know why it does not always work, though she does uphold the theory that "through toning, the body has the opportunity to slip into, and rest in, our perfect perfection" (Keys 28), or our true nature.

I've facilitated workshops with adults and teens using toning to increase self-awareness, and to enhance balance well-being. Toning is about presence and a personal expression of the sounds, flow, rhythm, and essence of the body's creative energy, expressed vocally. It is creativity in action, through the sounds that being created. Toning is literally the expression of who you are in the present moment, through the experience of your uniqueness. Toning is also about sharing. In a group setting, as each individual *tones*, they are expressing themselves uniquely in relationship to the group. As a collective, the participants directly experience unity within diversity kinesthetically. This is a form of *inner knowing*, is experienced through the body's wisdom. On a deeper level, toning is an opportunity to explore our uniquely creative nature, naturally, responsively, and collectively.

It may seem far-fetched to consider using toning in public schools. However, considering the lack of financial resources many districts face, schools may want to weigh the possibilities of introducing low-cost techniques that support a sense of well-being, such as toning, to students and staff. Students could find it empowering to take responsibility for their health without the use of harmful chemical substances they might be inclined to experiment with when feeling stressed. Toning is a naturally relaxing, yet invigorating way to get in touch with the body. Also, trying new experiences increases student's level of tolerance in refreshingly new ways.

Paul Newham is a sound-healing practitioner who developed a therapy based on the psychology of sound. Newham discovered nine ingredients of the voice, which can be explored to enhance a deeper understanding of our true nature: loudness, articulation, pitch, pitch fluctuation, register, harmonic timbre, violin, free air, and disruption. (Newham Audio).

Practices like toning help us see how willing we are to experiencing more holistic ways of learning. Toning could be presented as workshops in music and theater classes or used in English classes as a catalyst for creative writing and self- expose. Toning could even be presented in mathematics and physics classes as experiential lab experiments!

Listen, Learn, Relate

I had the extraordinary opportunity to participate in an interactive and dialectic weekend seminar in Cross Cultural Sound Healing with Dr. Pat Moffitt Cooke. One part of her seminar included listening to series of recordings from various cultures and asking the participants to document their experience while listening to the sounds. Cooke proposes that traumatic experiences we have encountered as children may result in a diminished capacity for the body to maintain the full range of frequencies that would keep it in balance. By re-introducing these harmonic frequencies, the body can regain a state of balance.

The following list describes the benefits of listening to music I received while attending Dr. Cooke's workshop. Numbers 1, 2, 4, 11, 12, 13, 15, and 17 on the following handout are demonstrated in the film, and most of the benefits were experienced in the film production. That's healing and creativity in action.

The Benefits of Using Music on a patient's emotional and mental state is far reaching. Here are a few benefits.

1. Stimulates attention and concern for one's inner life of feelings.
2. Provides a means of releasing pent-up emotions, dissipating tension, and expressing painful emotions.
3. Provides a means for containing uncontrolled impulses and feelings.

4. Provides a means for bringing unconscious feelings into consciousness so that thinking functions can begin.
5. Provides a means of bringing unconscious communication between two or more people.
6. Provides a means of bringing inner feelings into the outer world so they can be investigated and either accepted or rejected as part of the self.
7. Mobilizes and directs the flow of intuitive energy.
8. Provides a means of differentiating and integrating opposing feelings within the self.
9. Provides a means of expressing feelings which are often difficult to verbalize and thereby facilitates verbalization.
10. Provides a means of loosening up rigid or static feelings or attitudes and thereby induces dynamic change.
11. Reduces resistance against denied or spilt off emotions and allows them to be experienced.
12. Stimulates memories and images.
13. Prvides a non-verbal medium for interacting with visitors, therapists, and loved ones.
14. Provides a safe container and structure which encourages letting go of fears and inhibitions and facilitates play and mood elevation.
15. Provides a means of regulating and shifting between sensitivity to oneself and empathy with others.
16. Serves as a helpful third party in care giver-dying person or grieving person therapy.
17. Allows us to feel the depth of our sorrow, joy, peace, and unity with our divine.

(Pat Moffitt Cooke Ph.D., Kenneth Brucia, Ph.D.)

I try to practice deep listening skills as often as possible. Through my studies, I discovered that contemplative practices like meditation, yoga, transcendental drumming, chanting, and listening to the ragas of North India create a soundscape that supports a keener awareness of subtle energies, and vibration. When I'm in tune, I can hear harmonic overtones when a group sings monotone or when listening to repetitive drum rhythms and stringed instruments. Making it a practice to be clear in my thoughts, words, and intention has become powerful guide for determining whether my actions support the good of the whole. This practice can be applied to any setting and would be useful for faculty, administrators, and students.

Inviting students *and* staff to experiences that still the mind creates opportunity for mutuality and receptivity. These qualities innately assist our communication skills and our willingness to truly hear and respect others' points of view. This is key to organizing and structuring large institutions that are ultimately designed to serve all participants equally (such as school systems). Administrators, faculty, and students are equally vested in this experience. There is virtually no financial overhead in training staff and administrators in contemplative practices.

Supporting administrators and teachers in relational, introspective, and contemplative experiences empowers and enhances the adults charged with the task of instructing and administrating. As administrators relax into their innate response ability, they relate to faculty and staff as stewards. Relating becomes a mutually inclusive experience. Schools are then designed to be mutual, inclusive, and supportive of all participants.

The number of student disruptions in class became nearly non-existent after I introduced mindful meditation and relaxation response in class. In pausing, breathing, and feeling ourselves in relationship others, students and teachers can more fully respond. Teachers serve as guides, pointing students towards their uniquely creative, responsive abilities. Students are educated to become engaged, active citizens of the communities in which they serve.

John Beaulieu N.D., Ph.D. is an expert in sound therapy with an extraordinarily interdisciplinary background. Beaulieu's field of expertise spans across many fields including a classically trained musician, composer, professor, martial artist, consultant, and therapist. John has done groundbreaking work in sound healing therapies, bridging the gap between phenomenological research citing the therapeutic value of sound and healing and "hard" science, measuring the changes in the body's brain and chemistry with his development of *Biosonic Repatterning*. *Biosonic Repatterning* is "based on sonic ratios inherent in nature" used to balance the body and help it reach a state of homeostasis through entrainment, as the body's energy realigns with the intervals." (www.soundremedies.com).

In Beaulieu's first book, **Music and Sound in the Healing Arts,** John describes how he uses the five elemental sounds in his sound therapy, relating each element symbolically to an archetype or universal. Beaulieu explains that elemental sounds are *not* "good" or "bad," but "when the elements are suppressed, they will seek other forms of expression that may be unproductive to the individual" (Beaulieu 29). Beaulieu cites an example where a man will not raise his voice because of his fear of anger, resulting in excess fire energy, causing an ulcer. This theory reinforces my discussion in the beginning of Chapter Two concerning suppressed feelings and energy blockages. I suggest that if sound is used regularly in early training in schools as a preventative measure, it might help students feel safe in expressing their true feelings and make learning easier.

In his new book, **Human Tuning,** Beaulieu gives full detail of his theory and practice. John designed Fibonacci tuning forks, which tone precisely calibrated Pythagorean intervals to help the body maintain a state of balance and has been using them in his clinical practice for years. Sounding the tuning forks creates the harmonic ratio of a perfect fifth, measuring cycles of sound. This ratio is a "sonic beacon that resonates with the primordial wave of the universal energy field leading to the heart of stillness." (Beaulieu, 45). Interestingly, our bone joints are also connected in ratios, which resonate beautifully with the tuning forks when applied. (I can attest to this personally). Beaulieu describes in detail how the sympathetic (flight or fright) nervous system and the parasympathetic interact with one another signaling our muscles, bones and tendons and ligaments. The sound waves of the tuning forks resonate through our body, creating balance and wholeness.

I attended a symposium on Sound and Healing at Omega Institute in 2010, where John led a class describing his most recent research, in *Biosonics* and its consistent impact on brain synapses and the body's biochemistry, increasing levels of Nitric Oxide (NO) as a neurotransmitter and a locally acting hormone, reducing stress, and having a positive impact on disease. Recent studies in neuroscience are demonstrating that a relaxed, yet alert mind is ideal for learning.

John's brilliance does not overshadow his authenticity. His demonstration of wit, candor, approachability, and commitment to relate to his clients, workshop participants, and colleagues, is refreshingly inviting. In a conversation following the conference, John shared with me how he has introduced the tuning forks to several teachers in his son's school, and they use them in class (to reduce stress and help the students align their energy and gain focus.) Imagine how much fun it must be, exploring the tuning forks in school!

Caring for Yourself Leads to Caring for Others

I'd like to add a word or two here about teachers being guides in the process of contemplative practices across disciplines. Teachers like me who were intuitive children may have had the same experience I did during my formative years in school – that is, they may not have felt safe sharing their perceptual skills and may have coped by learned to compensate. During this process of adapting to the environment while needing to feel safe and belong, we learned to take care of other's need before our own. In many cases,

Guianese students performing Indian dances in the film shows how music and dance is the heart and soul of Indian and Guianese culture. The dance was one of many student-initiated performances that evening, which served as a fund-raiser for a child in the community in need of a hearing aide. We witness compassion in action through sound and celebration!

we "learned" that the needs of others are actually more important than our own needs. This idea is an inverted version of the truth!

SCHOOLS BENEFIT FROM TRAINING ADULTS TO BE CALM, FOCUSED, & BALANCED. We can then model these skills to students. Schools become a place where all children feel safe to be who they are and to explore their potential. Classrooms can offer the opportunity for students to develop the needed skills of rebalancing, refocusing, and redirecting their attention, and it is key that administrators support this course of action for the cycle to be complete. Students and teachers feel safe enough to be authentic and take notice of when they are out of balance, and – just as importantly -- learn how to return to a state of balance and inner calm. The pace and rhythm of the school day can -- and I believe *will*- support a balanced approach to learning.

Indigenous Cultural Perspectives on Music

In indigenous cultures, music is part of an elaborate intuitive oral tradition. Composing music is an active part of the entire life span. West African sound healer Yaya Dialog and Juan Namuncura, leader of the council of indigenous Argentines, both affirmed this concept during my internship through the Union Institute & University (UI&I). Both Dialo and Namuncura explained that song is a natural state of being which has nothing to do with the vocal quality of the person who creates the song. Songs are fashioned to describe daily activities and are also used during rituals and ceremonies, in celebrating new experiences, and in telling stories.

Larry Blumenfield, Ph.D. is a consultant for the United Nations Center for Human Rights. He has done extensive field research recording music of indigenous peoples across the globe in effort to help preserve these precious cultures. It has been common among the colonizing countries -- the United States, Canada, and New Zealand, for example -- to attempt to assimilate the indigenous population into the mainstream culture. Still, the indigenous peoples have found ways to maintain their identity through spiritual practices that are a part of their everyday life, their connection to nature, and through ceremony and rituals set apart from ordinary daily activities.

Westerners do not have easy access to this intuitive level of experiencing music. Native Americans in the United States who choose to remain loyal to their cultural and spiritual beliefs operate with "two different sets of values and behaviors, one for American culture and one for home" says L.A. Navajo singer, Arlie Neskahi (Blumenfield 72). What would schools be like if children were encouraged to write their own music, or have major input on the lessons of the day? How would our students' and teachers' lives change if they were given the opportunity to deeply explore the sounds, rhythms, and tones that they listen to? There is much to learn from our indigenous brothers and sisters concerning music opening our hearts to song creating opportunity for daily celebration.

The Magic Flute

For centuries, sound has been an extremely powerful tool used across cultures for healing purposes. Harmonics are intrinsic to devotional practices in many cultures. Jonathan Goldman discusses the use of harmonics in ancient times and the increased interest in their application today in an on-line interview, saying, "In the last decade, there has been increased awareness of the uses of sound and music as therapeutic modalities. I've attended and lectured at newly formed societies that are focused on merging science and the arts, particularly music. However, this use of sound and music to heal and transform actually dates back thousands of years, perhaps to the first uses of music itself. In the ancient mystery schools of Egypt, Athens, and Rome, for example, sound was understood

The footage that models using sound and rhythm for personal healing includes "Our Natural Rhythms" and "Sustainable Community." Both sections acknowledge the importance of becoming more in tuned with the natural harmonic flow of nature. These sections can be used to introduce a dialogue on this topic.

The background music, "Kill & Pachamama" in dreaming New Schools was written by Jorge Alfano. It was chosen to create a sonic feeling of connection supporting indigenous teachings. The footage demonstrates "music being used to explore relationships" and draws on aboriginal, Native American, African, African American, Latino, Guyanese, and Indian cultures.

to be the fundamental creative force of the universe. You can find knowledge of this in sacred texts of different traditions" (healingsounds.com).

Instruments like the indigenous flute show that ancient cultures have a profound understanding of the power of harmonics and their effect on states of consciousness. Other examples of these ancient meditation tools and shamanic instruments include Tibetan tingsha bells, Tibetan singing bowls, Native American rattles and drums, and Peruvian whistling vessels. These instruments carry a particular tonal quality that resonates with the harmonics that are found in the vibrating pulse of nature. The pulsing vibrations of sound waves have their roots in the cosmos.

Jorge Alfano is a master flutist, specializing in traditional South American and Tibetan devotional music, commissioned to play the flute for the Dali Lama in Florida, September 2004. In a telephone interview, I questioned him concerning the flutes he plays, wondering whether they are crafted with a specific intention, like the singing bowls and tingsha bells. Jorge explained that it depends on who carves the flute, but in ancient traditions of the indigenous people of the Andes, flutes were primarily crafted with the following three specific intentions:

(1) Flutes were often created to identify specific tones that correlated to a specific community or village of people used to communicate information.
(2) Flutes were crafted to synchronize with the stars at a given season. The use of astrology is intrinsic to Andean cosmology.
(3) Some flutes were created to be in tune with specific songs that were composed for royalty.

These ancient flutes are still played today. *When I heard the sweet sounds of the flute and the soothing sensation of their tones, I felt their deep resonance within my body.*

13 Native Peruvian Playing Flutes (J spring Dreamstime.com)

The fast-paced driving force that keeps schools operating is taxing on the mind, body, and spirit. I have experienced this first handedly, as have many of my students and co-workers. The tones created through indigenous flutes and other experiences in nature offer balance and receptivity to students and staff. Teaching students' facts about indigenous cultures is not nearly as far-reaching as giving them *experiences* of these cultures, which have the potential to change their perspectives in lasting ways. Students who have grown accustomed (and possibly addicted) to the fast-paced world that technology offers would benefit from experiencing the soothing harmonic tones of instruments like indigenous flutes. In addition, exposure to these sounds and the wisdom teachings that accompany them offers opportunity to explore our relationship to nature, as instruments like indigenous flutes are attuned to nature's sounds. In connecting with nature, students connect with themselves on a deeper level, naturally.

East Meets West: Indian Raga, Sanskrit & Mantra

In my doctoral studies, I couldn't help but notice that we all have certain tones that we naturally resonate with, reflected by the types of music that we enjoy listening to. Exposing students, staff, and administration to a wide range of cross- cultural sounds increases our awareness and understanding of one another -- a skill that is sorely needed in today's world! Schools would particularly benefit from respectfully offering inter-cultural exchanges through sounds and rhythms that they are not accustomed to, such as *mantras*, *chants*, and *raga*.

The word *mantra* comes from the Sanskrit roots *man* and *trai*, which translate to mind (or man), and liberation (or trai) device. In other words (quite literally), mantras are a system designed to liberate the mind. Many people confuse chants with mantras. Actually, mantras are words that are not vocalized, but thought or pictured in the mind (Ferrand audio). I use the term *mantra* to emphasize the power of the word, whether spoken or unspoken, but according to Vedic tradition, if the words are sung, the mantra becomes a chant.

Mantras are chanted in Sanskrit, which according to Vedic tradition, dates back to 6000 BCE. Sanskrit is known as the ancient language of the chakras. The Vedic, scientifically based spiritual formulas of mantra, were only taught by the Brahman Priesthood. This system teaches that using mantra can lead to spiritual evolution (Ferrand audio). Seed mantras are powerful one-syllable word mantras, which carry the essence of the entire mantra. Other Sanskrit words may be used to increase the capacity for the mantra to work effectively.

Virtually every writer on Indian music has struggled with the fundamental question of "What is a raga?" (Suvarnalata, Vander, and Harvey, introduction). We know that the term *raga* means "to color the mind," but the art form of raga is "far more precise and richer than a scale or mode, much less fixed than a particular tune" (Suvarnalata R., Vander M., and Harvey J) and "…it is a continuum with scale and tune as its extremes." (Suvarnalata, Vander, and Harvey).

Unlike mantras, where words are sung with the intention of invocation and devotion, no specific words are used in the singing of ragas. The intention to fully experience the notes sung in the body is, however, consistent in both mantra and raga. Monosyllables such as *Dai*, (pronounced die) and *sa* (pronounced sah) may be sounded in dhrupad (or vocal ragas) because the essence of the energy contained in the words is already present. However, it is not necessary to vocalize the words in order to capture their essence. (Dr. Ritwik Sanyal, internship).

Ragas may be sung and are commonly played on a double violin, sitar, or the bansuri, which is a traditional north Indian bamboo flute. Unlike the bright sounds of the classical flute, its tonal qualities are filled with woody overtones, like the flutes of Native North and South Americans. The sitar and esraj are fretless stringed instruments, which also produce circular harmonic scales rich with overtones.

A well-played raga can bring the listener to an altered state of consciousness. Sitar instructor Veena Chandra from Skidmore College, Saratoga Springs says that if you haven't dozed off at least once while listening to a raga, you are not relaxed enough to experience the raga.

14 Man Playing Sitar Scott Griessel, Dreamtimes.com

Specific ragas are sung or played at particular times of the day. The magical flavor of the raga resonates harmoniously with the quality of light of the specific time of the day, amplifying its potency. For example, an evening raga would have a different order of tones on the scale, which give the feeling of mystery in comparison with a morning raga.

I find raga to be an exceptional experience where I sense what I call "the space between the notes." These *micro-tonal* notes are embellished with slides as musician move gracefully up and down the scales of each raga. *As I listen with an open heart, I ride the waves of musical expression, and feel the essence of the music in my body, dancing in a sea of peaceful bliss. By allowing my body to melt into the musical experience I feel a sense of oneness and love that is difficult to describe.*

There is something unique about the harmonic structure of musical systems like raga that could certainly benefit schools. I have a personal connection to raga because I took the time to explore this system, in the US and India, however there are harmonic tonalities across cultures that produce similar brain activity, which in turn invite expansion, balance, and relaxation. Once again, being exposed to the sounds and rhythms of other cultures raises our awareness and increases tolerance as it gives a connecting point of reference to share, particularly in low-income communities where many children do not have the opportunity to experience the arts and cultural in ways that students from wealthier communities do. Harmonic systems, like raga, chanting, and mantra help the mind relax and ease into a contemplative state.

How do I envision the use of these soothing tones in the school and classroom? They could be piped into the hallways during passing time and used in the cafeteria and study halls. I use this practice regularly in my classroom and have noticed a major downward shift in the level of anxiety of students. Hearing cross cultural music expands our understanding and acceptance of other cultures. Music from each culture could be introduced from the early years and continue through high school to continually expose students to the sounds of our global community. Sound chambers could be developed to help students who have difficulty self-regulating or focusing their attention.

Drumming Into a Higher Consciousness

African music brings us closer to nature and speaks to the heart and soul of the community. Within the African drum culture there is a strong relationship between the drum, drummer, and dancer. Most drum rhythms are accompanied by song. A dialogue develops intuitively as the drummer and dancer interact through rhythm.

The *healing drum circle* is an ancient ritual comprised of drummers, dancers and singers creating harmonic tones and rhythms through song and drum. It is regarded with great respect, and the energy that is produced in ceremony is created by the cooperative efforts of the entire group led by the spiritual teacher/healer. There is a responsibility between all members of the community to honor the sanctity of the circle (Dialo seminar).

It's no surprise that drumming circles are being introduced to schools, community groups, and even and progressive business corporations to facilitate team building, communication skills, and enhance creativity. Drumming circles are an actively vibrant way to explore group dynamics as an integrated whole. Each participant adds to the richness of the sounds created as they cross cultural borders. In my experience, most teens and young children are intrigued and enlivened by the rhythms created through the sound of the drum. Because drumming is so richly kinesthetic, it is an easy avenue to release feelings and trauma, which are subconsciously stored in the body.

There are many stories of individuals who have been healed by the drum. Drumming brings us back to our natural rhythm and connects us with nature. The repetition of rhythms creates a sympathetic response in brain wave activity that is palpable. The energy flow in the body is increased. The drum rhythms each carry unique qualities that directly correlate to the elements, once again, naturally create a sense of well-being and balance. Teachers could be trained to use the drum as an interdisciplinary teaching tool to enhance self-reflection and creativity. Drumming is ideal for recreational time as well.

And as for stimulating the learning process? The problem for students, often, is that we ask them to access different parts of the brain at different times of the day, never giving their minds a chance to work as one unit of consciousness. Drumming can be used in classroom settings during transition periods or at times when there is a need to evoke a strong response from students who are stuck in a "holding pattern" where learning is blocked, so to speak.

I enjoy using music, drumming, chanting, and dance to clear energy and emotional blockages in my body. I feel the energy moving freely in my body as the blocked energy releases when I sing and move.

It feels wonderful to express myself freely.

I'm learning to simply allow my feelings to flow freely and grateful for the gifts I receive through this practice. I appreciate life's natural flow of events.

I believe this type of catharsis could be incredibly helpful, especially for secondary students struggling with issues of identity and angst. Because I've experienced this in my own life, I know the possibilities that sound, and rhythm offer for healing and the expansion of consciousness. I see the effect it has on students in my classroom. I've witnessed countless students,

The footage that models using sound and rhythm for personal healing includes "Our Natural Rhythms" and "Sustainable Community." Both sections acknowledge the importance of becoming more in tune with the natural harmonic flow of nature. These sections may be used to introduce a dialogue on this topic.

A researcher from the London Institute of Psychiatry, who had a cast on his arm dropped a notebook full of papers on the street. A second researcher was operating a lawn mower several hundred feet away. When the lawn mower was turned off, eighty percent of the bystanders stopped and helped pick up the dropped paper.

While the lawn mower was running, only fifteen percent of the bystanders stopped to help (Halpern cites Tarnopolsky, 92).

This experiment demonstrates how noise can affect states of consciousness or awareness.

teachers, staff, and administrators express their frustration in their futile attempts to adapt to the unhealthy rhythm of the school day. Consciously using sound, rhythm and music is a low-budget, easily accessible way to have a positive, sustaining impact on students and staff. It is also a great way to make learning fun!

Noise and Aggression

We've talked quite a bit about rhythm and sound in this chapter, but silence is also very important to the developing mind. "Our Natural Rhythms" reminds us of the importance of maintaining balance in our everyday lives by becoming more aware of the sounds that we are exposed to daily. Steven Halpern suggests that the noise level in our everyday lives is so pervasive, it knocks the body out of its natural rhythm. Halpern shares the story of composer John Cage, who chose a radical approach to demonstrate the value of silence by presenting a concert with a musical score that was entirely comprised of rest notes!

We each have different ideas about what we consider "noise." According to Halpern, noise can cause irritation, frustration, and aggravation. Halpern's lab experiments suggest that noise heightens a predisposition to anger and acting aggressively (Halpern). Given this information, it might be helpful to become aware of the aggressive noises we subject ourselves to, daily.

Soothing sounds from nature can help decrease anxiety and tension and give us energy. Nature calms our senses through color, sound, rhythm, smell, and stillness. Finding balance between the cacophonies of disharmonic sounds we expose ourselves to daily and those that bring balance can help us feel more peaceful and live more harmoniously.

In a scientific note, reaching deep states of relaxation-enhanced mind functioning results in increasing neuron size, the ratio of neuron synapses to neurons, and an increased ratio of glial cells to neurons formed. What this means to laymen is that relaxation – which usually implies an absence or minimization of noise, or the addition of the *right kind* of noise (keep reading) -- is essential for keeping the brain healthy. Through sound technology, an individual can reach the delta, deep meditative state. According to Harris, combining harmonic frequencies, which help the brain to function as a synchronized whole, rather than two lateralized sides has created unified brain wave movement similar to that of yogi masters who have practiced meditation for decades such as Swami Rama, a research patient studied in 1970 by Elmer Green, Ph.D. (We'll talk more about the syncing of the brain hemispheres in Chapter 8.)

Synchronization of brain waves raises the individual threshold to more conscious responses to external stimuli, which would normally cause stress. I use a combination of ancient and very new systems, which help me return to a state of balance more consistently and bring greater clarity. They include practicing stillness in my active daily schedule, silent meditation, listening to and playing drums and other instruments, which create circular harmonic resonant fields, used in ancient meditative practices, and running the light body (energy body) frequencies I learned through my internship. Continued research in these fields of study and how they can relate to the classroom is needed, but I think it stands to reason that encouraging students to take the time to be silent every now and then – through meditation and/or through the use of harmonic frequencies – could have a very positive effect on teen brain development and their interpersonal interaction.

Chapter Eight

"Everything in the universe has a rhythm, everything dances."
Maya Angelou

Using Elemental Energies, Rhythm, and Movement to Support Focus and Balance

As Joachim Earnest Berendt explains, science teaches that the phenomenon of entrainment is universal: "Two oscillators pulsating in the same field in almost identical rhythm will tend to lock in with result that eventually their vibrations will become precisely synchronous … this phenomenon is known as phase locking or entrainment" (Berendt 116). Berendt himself observes that as students become more sensitive to the harmonious rhythms of other cultures, they are guided towards listening more compassionately, developing cultural awareness and feelings of connection.

The really amazing thing about entrainment is that it can open the brain to new ways of processing stimuli and information, and it can also change the body's response to over-stimulation and other stressors. In short, entrainment doesn't change the world around us – just the way we see it and handle it.

In Vedic tradition, the Bija Mantra is considered the "vibrational frequency" that the energy of the body (which is contained in the chakras) vibrates at. While energy swirls in the chakras at all times, the Bija is the *latent* energy at each chakra point which can be coaxed out and brought to life, so to speak, by certain sounds called seed syllables.

The five elements (earth, water, fire, air, and space) are intrinsically connected to the seed syllables. Each of the five energy centers in the body carries the essence of the corresponding elements. The Vedic tradition teaches that our bodies are one with nature in that they are both made of the elements and supported *by* the elements. Health and well-being are experienced when our energy centers are in balance and harmonious with nature's elements.

Moving from the base to the crown …

- The first energy sound is *Lang* (pronounced lung), which represents the elemental sound of earth.
- The second center's sound is *Vang* (pronounced vung), representing water.
- The sound of the third energy center is *Rang* (pronounced rung), representing fire.
- The fourth energy center 's sound is *Yang* (pronounced yung), which represents air.
- The fifth chakra responds to the sound *Hang* (pronounced hung), the sound of space.
- *Aum* (pronounced *ah-oh-oom*) is the sound of light and is associated with the sixth chakra.
- The seventh chakra is the realm of purest and most subtle consciousness and is represented by silence.

According to Vedic teachings, as these energy centers are awakened, the energy rises and the individual reaches a state of supreme consciousness, awakening parts of the brain that normally lie dormant. Through entrainment (which we will discuss in the following section), the energy systems throughout the body become increasingly more balanced, thereby increasing the capacity to experience a complete energetic balance.

Using Elemental Energy Rhythm and Movement for Maintaining Focus and Balance

Entrainment is universally found in nature -- and it is so ubiquitous, we hardly notice it. One such example would be observing a flock of birds in flight. Boston scientist William Condon notes "two people engaged in a good conversation are experiencing entrainment." I would describe this experience as sharing harmonic resonant fields of energy. John Beaulieu describes this process as one of "merging with the pulse of the music" (Beaulieu 70). We can achieve this state by relaxing the body and allowing it to feel the beat. Through practice, we can reap the benefits of the repetitive rhythms.

Behavioral Kinesthetic Psychiatrist John Diamond did a series of muscle tests using different drum rhythms and determined that there were "good rhythms" and "bad rhythms." For example, according to Diamond, the rhythms of hard rock and heavy metal placed the down beat in the beginning of the stanza, which creates a "jump effect," breaking a continuous loop of rhythm, thereby causing the body to experience stress. Meanwhile, "good rhythms" reflect the beating of the human heart, which places the upbeat in the beginning of the stanza, thereby causing a relaxation response (Diamond). Heartbeat rhythms have been used in NICU units to soothe preemies and have been proven to be quite effective in calming infants (Cooke). Programs like heart math can help students who struggle with with attention and emotional difficulties by supporting heart coherence.

Clinical Application of Entrainment

The five elements were a large part of the training I had during my doctoral internship in multi-cultural sound healing practices and Andean spirituality in Urubamba, Peru. The two weeks spent in Peru included visiting sacred sites in Cusco, Urubamba (the Inca Valley) and Match Pichu. Cultural anthropologist, award winning author, educator, and consultant for the Fetzer Institute, Angeles Arrien describes an entrainment practice that Native South Americans use when they are fearful and choose to stabilize and refocus their attention. They would use a combination of chanting and body movements to bring the situation to new light. I learned two chants that were amplified with full body gestures; designed to bring the qualities of the five elements into the body, to increase awareness and perception, and bring light to the body, mind, and spirit.

Pat Moffitt Cooke teaches toning the seed syllables or (Bija mantras), another form of entrainment, in her weekend intensive in multicultural sound healing. I found chanting the seed mantras in group to be a powerful experience. During my session, several people were moved by the physical and emotional response that their body had in chanting, especially when the group chanted the primordial sound of ancient Sanskrit *aum*. Participating in like-minded group energy augmented my experience of feeling the vibrations of the Bija mantras in my body. I noticed that the chakras felt revitalized and energized when I focused my attention on them as I chanted the mantras. I experienced and heard many overtones vibrating in my body when the *aum* was chanted.

Brain Hemispheres, Intuition & Creativity

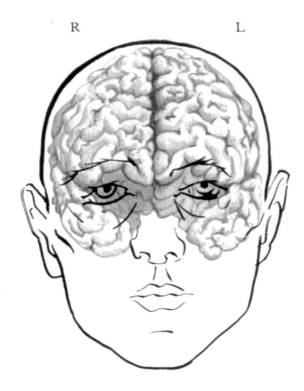

R   L

15 brain

The right side of the brain functions as the creative center, "the seat of visual, aural, and emotional memory," it "processes information in holistic, intuitive terms, relying on pattern recognition" (Redmond 172). This is the part of the brain that facilitates the creative process of becoming a musician.

Meanwhile, "the left brain is the administrator, what we sometimes call the rational mind. It proceeds in logical, analytical, verbal, and sequential fashion. Incoming information is identified, classified, and explained here" (Redmond 172). And, as I mentioned earlier in this chapter, the two sides of the brain not only operate in different modes, but they also usually operate at different rhythms; for example, "the right brain may be operating in alpha waves, while the left brain is in beta state" (Redmond 173). Or both hemispheres may be generating the same type of brain waves but be completely out of sync with one another. Redmond continues, "in states of intense creative or deep meditation, or under the influence of rhythmic sound, both hemispheres may begin operating in the same synchronized rhythm" (Redmond 174). In other words, rhythmic entrainment has the capacity to assist in brain synchronization, strengthening each hemisphere.

Incorporating intuitive, non-linear teaching models within a linear system poses some challenges, but it can be done (popular programs used in schools such as the Mind Gym support this theory), and this is exactly what I am proposing through holistic learning models which include the entire body and mind in the learning process, supporting the belief that the body and mind can work as a collaborative intelligent whole!

Here's where the idea of brain hemispheres and rhythm gets interesting: In states of intense creativity, or deep meditation, or under the influence of rhythmic sound, both hemispheres experience what is called hemispheric synchronization, or unified- whole brain functioning (Redmond, 173). If the brain is synchronized at the alpha wavelength, deep states of deep mental clarity, euphoria and intense creativity can be experienced. Rhythmic movement can also affect the brain because each hemisphere controls the motor skills of one half the body.

A fascinating livestream available on TED.com, called *A Stroke of Insight,* by Jill Bolt Taylor, Ph.D. clearly demonstrates this phenomenon. Music has been shown to enhance brain function. Drumming may be one the best ways to develop brain synchronization, since it carries the qualities of music, rhythm, and full body involvement.

Neurological studies indicate that the brain hemispheres develop as one and at approximately age five, each side of the brain begins to specialize. I find it interesting to note that although we have one brain, the terminology that scientists use to describe the brain would imply that there are indeed two *different* brains: a left brain, and a right brain! Isn't it time to make sure we are reaching and educating both sides?

Entrainment through Drumming

In 1998, I participated in an intensive study of frame drumming with the late Layne Redmond and twenty participants, entitled *Giving Birth to Ourselves.* The group met one weekend a month for six months, and participants studied over an extended period of time to process the learning experience and practice drumming between instructional weekends. There was a common thread between my personal experience, and that of the collective group, which can be seen in the picture included in the following section.

16 (Giving Birth to Ourselves Intensive, Cairo, NY 1998)

Our beautiful drumming group experienced the positive effects of rhythmic entrainment, becoming energized yet stilled by the drum, depending on the rhythms played and the focus or intention of the instruction being presented. The natural flow of the learning process was inspiring. I discovered my precision, speed, and timing was much better with the group than any experience I had drumming alone. What most amazed me was the level of personal growth that each woman experienced through the six months of training. We shared our stories over meals, during breaks, on walks, and in the evening when the full day of training was completed.

I continued my studies in an advance training weekend with Layne and several of the women from the initial training session in the fall of 2004. (Footage is shown in Dreaming New Schools.) Layne was a gracious teacher with a heart of gold, who passed away in 2013. It was remarkably inspiring that I could leave a learning community and return years later, still sensing incredible connection and creativity through the drum circle.

Master drummer and sound healer Yaya Dialo noted that many Western drummers primarily lead (or favor) one hand, rather than using both hands ambidextrously. He used his fingers to demonstrate a person walking, left foot forward to right foot, rather than a smooth left, right gait, saying this is how Americans use our bodies, unconsciously. Dialo implied we are out of rhythm and do not realize it. *It is as though our left and right sides of the brain do not know how to collaborate completely*, which, of course, they most probably don't, since our schools are set up to primarily strengthen the left side and leave the right side asleep at the wheel (or drum, as it were).

Drum cultures such as African or Brazilian cultures recognize the power of the drum and the sanctity of its use. Redmond described her first encounter with a drum culture – it was 1980, and she was asked to lead a drumming workshop where master drummers from Brazil would be in attendance. Redmond explained that the drum was considered sacred in many ancient cultures, and she proceeded to demonstrate her drumming techniques using the drum to honor the divine feminine. The male Brazilian drummers honored and respected her work, and the entire group played together, improvising wonderful rhythmic melodies. Why am I sharing this particular story? It's a significant point to consider -- intention plays in the use of the drum in creating community. When there is no judgment, no right or wrong, only openness and feeling in a group, our energy flows freely and binds us to one another.

Drumming also played a pivotal role in my discovering my voice. As I became more practiced, I played more intuitively without concentrating on the particular rhythms. I discovered that vocal melodies were easily created from my internal body's mechanism while I was drumming – I was accessing and really using that right side of my brain with ease! This was particularly true when I intuitively thought of a prayer or sacred verse I had previously memorized. Spontaneously, the words that expressed my feelings would flow and the rhythms and melody were in synchronization with the drum rhythms being played. Chants became a platform for me to explore my musical capacity by playing with rhythms and tones. Singing them created a feeling of peacefulness, creation, and completion.

Why would I recommend drumming as a means of reaching at-risk students? For starters, rhythmic movement and drumming is perhaps one of the most effective ways to develop both left and right brain, according to Redmond. But also, I know what this process has done for me personally, and for those in the workshops alongside me. Embracing my inner musician increased my level of self-confidence and helped me re-discover my voice. It taught me to listen more deeply. I became more articulate in my speech patterns and more aware of the tonal quality that I used (for example, there was a time when I could be quite sarcastic, particularly with my high school students). As my listening skills increased, I began to explore the emotions that lay dormant behind that sarcasm, and I recognized that it was a response to feeling disempowered. Acknowledging this gave me the opportunity to communicate more authentically with my students. I practiced more effective discipline techniques in the classroom and no longer needed a sharp tongue to reel my students in.

This learning experience was not linear. It seemed to move like a spiral, excitingly colorful and fluid, and constantly changing as new information was experienced and processed. I could observe and feel the changes in my attitudes and behaviors, but I did not have a bar graph to place them on. They were much more like the diagrams in Buzan's text, which I would best describe as flowering states of awareness that come from within the center of my being.

17 Flowering Rose

Adolescent Brain Development, Entrainment, and Personal Growth

Anyone who has worked with young adults has witnessed the conundrum of internal and external emotionally fueled experiences that they adjust to daily. And while we may able to sympathize and/or empathize with them, we have to remember that their experiences are far different from adult traumas. The pre-frontal cortex is the part of the brain responsible for reason, judgment, and self-discipline. The adolescent brain is not fully developed and is constantly in flux as it shapes personality and behavior. In plain language, adolescents do not have the life experience or fully formed brain development that we, as adults, have hopefully acquired to help mitigate the emotional upheavals in life. Practicing mindfulness throughout the school day can help student's capacity to focus and learn to become the objective observer of stressful experiences they face daily, and even develop social confidence. In short, they can develop the tools or inner muscles to become reflective, and self-empowered decision makers. We also know that the earlier this process begins, the better the results. Schonert-Reichl, -Molly Stewart Lawler)

Every teen goes through a period of adjusting to their changing body and mind, and it's rarely a simple or painless process. Teens having no counsel in self-determination and healthy decision-making skills, however, are at risk for making choices that are destructive, such as drug experimentation and/or use. Instructing young adults to be respectful of and comfortable with their changing bodies may alleviate some of the confusion that they experience.

As you will see demonstrated in Dreaming New Schools: contemplative practices, nature, sound, music, and entrainment through rhythm can all help to ease this process.

Witnessing the positive effects of using relaxation techniques in my classroom on a regular basis made me keenly aware of the profound opportunity for students to work with teachers who were trained in in mindfulness, and self-reflective skills. It was years later that I learned that there was hard science supporting what I sensed intuitively. The increased levels of cortisol to the pre-frontal cortex, helps increase attention, and increased levels of serotonin, improves the social/ emotional state of being through the practice of mindfulness.

Dr. Jon Kabat Zinn began his research in mindfulness and its impact on stress, emotional hardiness in 1982 at the University of Massachusetts Center for Mindfulness in Health Care, Medicine, and Society. His long-standing research demonstrates that mindfulness practiced over time increases in grey matter density, helping them act "effectively under stress". You can visit the MBSR website for more juicy research. Gina Biegel's Stress Reduction Workbook for Teens is a wonderful teaching tool.

Mind Mapping and Sensory Learning

Mind mapping is an innovative system of utilizing the brain's capacity developed by Tony and Barry Buzan. (I find it to be so helpful, I used a mind map to conceptualize my doctoral thesis.)

Mind maps are visual constructs used to conceptualize ideas. They begin with a central idea with related ideas branching off. They can take many forms, including pictures, words, or symbols. A crude, but helpful mind map I used to conceptualize my dissertation is seen on the right.

18 My Mind Map for Doctoral Thesis

According to research, during the learning process, the human brain primarily remembers the following:

- Ideas from the beginning of the learning period
- Ideas from the end of the learning period
- Any ideas which are of particular interest to the person
- Any ideas associated with things or patterns already stored in memory
- Any ideas which are emphasized as being in some way outstanding or unique
- Any ideas which appeal particularly strongly to any of the five senses (Buzan 29)

The last four characteristics on the list demonstrate that the use of rhythmic and or musical entrainment exercises increase the brain's capacity for remembering, particularly with teens. Patterns stored in our memory, for example, can be accessed at a later point in time. Entrainment reinforces this process.

The learning process can be further enhanced by layering visuals such as mind maps with the use of rhythmic or musical entrainment and bodily kinesthetic experiences. The examples in the preceding section indicate that the brain may be entrained using rhythm. Further investigation using rhythmic musical input as a sensory practice may enhance the learning experience.

Using Harmonics, Sound, and Rhythm for Personal Transformation

♪ π

Synchronization of brain waves raises the individual threshold towards conscious responses to over stimulation, which would normally cause stress.

How can sound, rhythm and music be used for personal growth in a learning community? Bill Harris, Ph.D. has combined meditation practices with neurochemistry and sound technology at the Centerpointe Research Institute and discovered that deep states of meditation and relaxation foster mind growth, resulting in increased clarity, intelligence, creativity, intuition, and joy.

Reaching deep states of relaxation enhances mind function, resulting in increased neuron size, an increased ratio of neuron synapses to neurons, and an increased ratio of glial cells (which support and nourish brain cells) to neurons formed. Through sound technology, the individual can reach the delta (or deep, deep) meditative state where the tension between opposites may be transcended. According to Harris, combining harmonic frequencies assists the brain in functioning as a synchronized whole, rather than two lateralized sides. This results in unified brain wave movement similar to that of yogi masters who have practiced meditation for decades. Through changes in the individual's alpha, beta, and theta states of awareness, the brain is stimulated to escape into a higher order, as Harris explains: "while the limitations of the old system's way of seeing things keeps us from evolving to the next level, reaching deep meditative states purifies the filter in which we see the world" (Harris CD intro).

Meditation and entrainment create circular harmonic resonant fields used in ancient meditative practices. Using the light-body frequencies learned through my internship also creates a circular flow of energy in the body that results in mental clarity, energetic balance, and peaceful sensations. These systems all apply the theory of harmonics in some way.

As Multi-Dimensional Creative Beings, we have the capacity to influence our habitual, destructive patterns through our interactive forms of devotion, kinesthetic experiences recorded in the body that create a sense of

Music has been recognized as a gateway to transformation for centuries.

Anthony Storr suggests that Nietzsche may have understood music better than any other philosopher, recognizing:

(a) music as art can reconcile one to life and enhance one's life

(b) music is physically and emotionally based, and rooted in the body &

(c) music is transformative.

Storr explains that in music, one can feel raptured by a power greater than himself, almost God like.

Music carries both an internal and external quality of greatness, as we hear it, and feel it kinesthetically in our body.

balance such as rhythmic entrainment and silence and contemplation. I also suggest that by mindfully practicing the use of our intellect and conscious creativity, we can bring our brain into synchronization, strengthening the hemispheres predominantly responsible for these processes.

The following narrative describes a musical encounter I had with a man I met a few years back. This experience was like Storr's oceanic response -- transcending ordinary reality. It shows sound being used as the catalyst for the intuitive process of balancing intellect and intuition, resulting in personal growth as seen in the CPPT. It also demonstrates the magical qualities of music that I mention the introduction of Dreaming New Schools.

John Michael and I met in Burlington, Vermont, on a warm summer day some time ago. An extraordinary experience happened while we were sitting together on a park bench discussing the power of sound. As I was humming and playing the doumbek (a Middle Eastern drum), John Michael spontaneously began chanting a series of Indian Vedic chants. The Hindu words flowed from his tongue with ease. John Michael continued chanting for several minutes. While he sang, I felt a circle of energy flow from my heart to his. It cycled around continuously while he chanted, and I played my drum. It felt as though my heart became a conduit for the circular current of energy that flowed between us. This experience enriched my understanding of devotion. Peaceful, blissful, serenity moved gently through both of us as he chanted and I hummed along, playing my drum. I asked John Michael when he had studied Vedic chanting, and he responded that he had no prior knowledge of Vedic chants, but on rare occasions "channeled" the prayers. These "channeled" prayers seemed to come from nowhere. If the prayers are seen as extensions of the physical body through intention, beyond space and time then perhaps John Michael was "tuning in" to a harmonic frequency that resonated with his energy field.

Music lovers like me will continue to use sound and rhythm as a means to explore the world. It is my hope that our learning experiences become magical, enlightening exchanges of creative enterprise through further research and integration of harmonics in our schools.

Technology's Effect on our Internal Rhythm

Students expect immediate responses, spending hours a day on electronic devices. It's no wonder their attention spans have been impacted. People have become culturally entrained to be easily distracted, and since the average American household uses electronic devices at least four to six hours daily, we're talking about a lot of distracted students not fully experiencing the moment-to-moment events that shape their minds and hearts!

Guiding students to become more fully present is a life skill. Amazingly, this skill is possible through the simplest of experiences, which require absolutely no financial risk for schools. It does, however, require shifting our orientation towards learning to recognize and value mutually progressive ways of being and understanding that learning occurs most fully through direct experience. Consciously following our breath and practicing mindfulness through a variety of contemplative forms such as meditation, yoga, tai chi, drumming, singing, toning, chanting, or dancing are just a few examples of opportunities schools could offer to their participants. Key to each of the practices mentioned is the understanding of non-judgment. It is not about getting the yoga or breathing right, but much more about continually opening to our innate receptivity as a gentle process, naturally. The body's response to these practices is cumulative as it eases into its uniquely balanced internal rhythm. As the body entrains, it becomes receptive to its natural state of joy and inner peace. Those who facilitate these experiences would naturally do so relationally, holding the reverence for human life that was described in chapter one.

Contemporary research using rhythm and entrainment can be continued for children who are easily distracted. Guiding students in identifying their

Teaching students to self- regulate is a skill that would benefit many. The modalities mentioned above are viable sources for developing this ability. The Raven Drum Foundation supports sound, movement and rhythm used in educational settings for healing (www. ravenfoundation.org).

Our after-school program's Michael Jordan Grant Drum Circle created community. The circle helped a diverse group of students develop confidence, ease and authenticity, drumming, singing, and sharing original songs and rhythms. Peers became friends. Some students performed at our High School Poetry Jam. Now that's what I call transformative learning!

obsessive behaviors and thoughts is an extremely valuable skill. Many students classified with ADD or ADHD have not been given structure and a means to observe and modify disruptive behavior patterns.

Healing Sounds and Rhythms and My Personal Journey

Early years in Catholic school were traumatic as you can imagine, being a sensitive child who dreamed of magic carpets and houses filled with jewels. My childhood was overshadowed with Guardian Angels and, huge dark churches with red velvet confessional curtains, Lord I am not worthy prayers, holy communion, screaming kindergarten teachers, and nuns who wore habits and carried rulers. The contrast was so difficult for me, I subconsciously blocked out many of my early school memories in defensive response. Guilt, fear, shame, and humiliation were the law of the land in parochial school where corporal punishment was still in full force. There were rumors that some junior and senior high school administrators in the public school used paddles on male students who were "out of line". The rumor was enough to keep the girls and most baby boomer boys in line, although I knew they weren't rumors.

Individuals who do not follow the consenting group are often ostracized until they either leave the group, physically or emotionally. Though sometimes, they conform to the group standard as you can see in the conclusion of Dreaming New Schools. I discovered that fear, guilt, shame, and humiliation are sensory experiences that are not only felt, but also held in the body if the initial trauma is not released. Pat Moffitt Cooke and Bob Harris are doing groundbreaking work in this field using harmonics and sound to bring emotional wounds to the surface, where they can be released and replaced with affirming beliefs.

Sound, rhythm and music have served as catalysts for my personal growth. Each has the capacity to evoke emotions because they are sensory experiences. Once I became aware of my emotions and the core beliefs that have influenced my limited perception of reality, I was able to release those limiting beliefs. You can see this in the conclusion of the film in a wave of emotional, as I come to the realization that I didn't fit into the predominant model of intelligence as a child. Expressing these emotions was so difficult that there were great pauses in my statement: "When I was a child [...] I did not think that I was [...] smart, intelligent [...] and that I had the capacity to learn [...]" In that moment I realized for the first time that I did not see myself as intelligent because creativity was not considered an authentic assessment of intelligence.

A conscious intention to use sound, rhythm, and music for healing, using my auditory, kinesthetic, and intuitive learning style has supported my self-confidence and personal growth. This is clearly shown in the classroom scene "when I was in school [...]" and "Personal Transformation", where I share my creative process through mantra-like thoughts integrated as a voice-over. My personal experience of the following creative processes led to change within myself for the better (creativity, contemplation, self-reflection, disclosure, vulnerability, integrity, self-awareness).

Because sound, rhythm and music are three of my greatest passions, they have become an extremely powerful means of expressing my creativity. For example, listening to my body, taking breaks, and following my need to play music, sing, dance, chant, or drum helped me feel more balanced in my studies and the completion of the film and dissertation without suffering through exhaustion, anxiety, or frenetic and obsessive belief patterns. Integrating sound, music, and rhythm into the research process in the contextual essays fueled, soothed, and nurtured my creative spirit. Further research in art therapy and arts in education can help bridge the gap between the artist-teacher-researcher and artist-art therapist-researcher to facilitate the transition of applying an individual learning experience into group settings.

My learning cycle literally came full circle as I filmed the conclusion of Dreaming New Schools. In the introduction I dedicate the film to the students whose learning styles don't fit into the norm. I was thinking of the courageous students that I encounter each day at Schenectady High School when I wrote that script. I did not think of myself being included in that group!

Experimental Pilot Programs Using Sound, Rhythm, and Movement

I would love to see the development of pilot programs using music to support a relaxation response in primary and secondary schools. Classroom passing time could be more relaxed, with the appropriate musical interludes being played. Students would also become more aware of cross-cultural sounds if multicultural music was selected and used in curriculum with regularity. Soothing music could be played to students before a peer mediation session, giving them time to redirect and calm themselves.

Drumming, and music are natural catalysts for releasing tension and stress and could be used to help release feelings that require more "fire" to let go of. Students would have the opportunity and satisfaction of self-correcting, instilling a sense of pride before they meet with the person they are in conflict with. Soothing sounds can also be used when a soft focus is needed to accomplish a task.

There are many variables to consider when using entrainment for self-regulating, increasing focus, and maintaining balance, including:

- Cultural preference of sounds, rhythms, and intonations
- The amount of energy the student exhibits
- The type of learning required during a particular assignment

Individual sound stations (or chambers) for use under adult supervision could also be made available for students, providing a variety of harmonic resonant fields for students to immerse themselves. (For example, if a student needs fire energy for invigoration, they may listen and dance to the drum rhythms of the African djembe or the Middle Eastern Doumbek. Both drums carry a high-pitched timbre, but the rhythmic melodies vary quite a bit.). Some chambers could provide room for movement. Classes using movement such as Tai Chi, Yoga, Belly Dance, Hip Hop, and African Dance could be available to relieve stress and bring energy into the body. Students could use the chamber to experience cultural diversity, which would enhance lessons in content areas such as history and social science.

Reflections on Personal Transformation Using Sound

I've discovered that in personal transformation, there is a profound connection between the heart and the mind. In this process, consciousness is awakened as they reach a new level of understanding or realization about themselves and how they relate to others and the world around them. *In my case, there was a "softening of the heart" and a "fluidity" of the mind and its thought processes.*

My journey through multi-cultural and cross-cultural sounds, and the cultures that express these sounds, became a doorway to experience the world in a new way. One of the most profound changes in my worldview was realized through sound as I became increasingly open to other cultural ways of being. I came to understand sound as a harmonic unifying field of energy. Surrendering my thought process and listening to the sounds of other cultures with my entire body helped me to experience the harmonic frequencies more fully. Through the soundscape, my ego melts away, giving my body the pleasure of experiencing the new without constraints. I simply experience being in the creative process of immersion. I experience and appreciate the beauty of unity within diversity, through sound.

My heart and mind are learning to work together as I embrace my innate child-like nature with curiosity and willingness to explore new cultural and sonic experiences without judgment. When I release my inner judgments and concerns about others' approval, I am free to mindfully explore - sonically, culturally, intellectually, emotionally. This newly found freedom creates inspiration, joy, and new life energy that is palpable, which I can share with my students!

The narratives in section text explore an experience of energy vibration innate to life, which either changed my perspective or created a kinesthetic healing response in my body supporting inclusiveness and wholeness. I discovered a different purpose for my mind than the one that I had been previously trained to see.

I find that the power of my mind is most potent when I am fully present with the activity I'm engaged in, free to choose where to focus my attention. I practice stilling my mind through contemplative practices, engage my body in sound, rhythm, or silence. When I'm in that zone, I feel my mind, body, and creative spirit as one, in union. And by this, I mean physically. Like bubbles in champaign, my energy flows freely, the two states of being cannot be separated interacting with one another.

I've also discovered that developing an awareness of the interactions between my body, mind, and spirit is a practice that can be cultivated through focused intent. For me, the key to this experience is choosing to be heart-centered, a wise choice that places love, and acceptance above all. It's a process of surrendering old beliefs of separation, limitation, fear, and lack.

Silence combined with breath creates a harmonic wave like the peaceful bliss I sometimes experience while chanting. As a practice, experiencing harmony becomes easier over time. It's cumulative, and like riding a bicycle -- once the body has recorded its response, it can never be fully forgotten. I have practiced this technique for many years. Our bodies love feeling relaxed. And relaxation response is a real thing. We can experience tranquility through continued contemplative practices, even if we have been away from the practices for some time. Walking in nature, listening to music, drinking a cut of tea, humming, or simply sitting and breathing can bring us back to center. What a gift to offer to our youth – a means of using their own bodies and minds to quell stress and over-stimulation, and a skill they can carry with them for the rest of their lives.

Chapter Nine

"Sometimes the questions are complicated, and the answers are simple."
Dr. Seuss

What Do the Students Have to Say?

I thought it would be interesting to give you a look at what my inner-city students are dealing with and responding to on a day-to-day basis. As you will see, today's youth are faced with some serious stressors coming from all sides – home, school, society, you name it. But there are also some wonderful opportunities for these students to see other, holistic learning experiences and the world that awaits them, and I have been fortunate enough to witness the transformation that comes along with the completion of these programs.

Student-Focused Surveys

In 2011 and 2012, I taught a "Children in Crisis course, part of the holistic curriculum offered at our High School. It was designed to help students see themselves as student- leaders and agents of change, while exploring contemporary issues that may place children at risk or in crisis. Intervention is key to the course and students share what they have learned with peers in a variety of forms including local field trips to suburban schools, and small assembly programs at our high school.

Students in two of my "Contemporary Issues and Children in Crisis" classes developed and conducted a survey concerning high school students and education as part of their research project on addressing the value of intervention in times of crisis. The students were interested in determining whether their peers felt that schools were in crisis and in need of change and they also wanted to know what their peers believe schools can do to better serve the needs of students. All of the students who participated in conducting the survey agreed that it was important to get input from their peers. They felt validated and saw themselves as agents of change in communicating their concerns with others.

It is vitally important to hear from the students and understand their perspectives on learning and the environment in which it takes place. The survey questions and results are reflective of the insight that teens have concerning their surroundings, values, and goals. It's important for us, as educators, parents, and administrators to interpret the responses with open minds.

There were two parts to the survey. The first part consisted of the following yes-or-no questions:

1. Do you think public schools are in a state of crisis?
2. Do schools prepare students for their life goals?
3. Are schools ideally designed for learning?
4. Are there subjects that should be taught in school that are currently not offered?
5. Are standardized tests an accurate assessment of what students are learning?
6. Do you know someone who lives in a group home/
7. Do you know someone who is in foster care?
8. Have you been satisfied with the amount of personal attention you have received in school?
9. Have you ever cheated on a test?

The second part of the survey was comprised of student- driven short-answer questions:

1. What are the biggest challenges students in our high school face?
2. Have you benefited from being in school? If so, how?
3. Why do you attend school?
4. What would an ideal school setting look like?
5. What other ways could student's achievements could be measured more accurately?
6. Do you feel that schools should be responsible for students in need of emotional support? How so?
7. Why do students cheat on tests?
8. I wish schools _____.

The students used these questions along with the questions from Part One to generate discussion with fellow classmates. Here are the results from the survey, as compiled by the students:

- More than half of the students felt that public schools were in a state of crisis.
- Nearly half of the students did not feel that schools prepared them for their life goals.
- One-third felt that schools were set up ideally for learning.
- Three-fourths felt that there were courses that should be offered in school that were not available.
- Three-fourths of respondents felt that standardized tests did not accurately assess what students had learned in school.
- More than half the students interviewed knew someone who lived in a group home, and two thirds knew of someone who lived in foster care.
- Two-thirds were satisfied with the amount of personal attention they receive in school.
- Three-fourths of the students had cheated on at least one test.
- The greatest challenges the teens interviewed faced included attending school, society, friends, pregnancy, violence, peer pressure, drugs and alcohol, laziness, gangs, home life, sex, and money (listed in order of priority).
- When asked how school had benefited students, the most common answer was learning new skills (nearly half the students stated so); one-sixth listed meeting people as a benefit; one-sixth said they had not benefited at all; four students stated that they had grown emotionally, while three students stated that school kept them out of trouble.
- A little more than half of the students stated that they come to school to learn.
- One-third of the students interviewed attend school to prepare for their future goals.
- One-sixth stated that they attended school to prepare for college. One-twelfth attended for their parents or because they had to. Other answers included seeing friends, unsure, to discover who they are, or to have something to do. One student comes to school for sports.

* Note: The number of students who knew of peers who were in foster care or who live in *group homes* may seem alarming to some, but I would imagine that it is quite common in school districts who serve children of low-income families. The student's responses raise some serious questions concerning the unique needs of students who are under the State's care, and whether traditional schools can meet the educational needs of students who are dealing with huge emotional upheaval as a common occurrence in their daily life.

The responses to the short answer questions were as follows:

- Students want to be in schools that are attractive, safe, non-violent, student-centered, and clean. They want smaller classes, and want to do things they care about, with less structure and more freedom.
- When asked how student assessments could be more representative of student achievement, students suggested personal interviews, class participation being counted rather than state assessments, opportunities for critical analysis, and teacher evaluations based on student growth and projects.
- Students surveyed were not as clear in their viewpoint as to whether schools should be responsible for student's emotional growth. Nearly half of the students surveyed were indecisive or did not answer this question. Of the remaining fifty percent, two-thirds felt that schools should be responsible for student's emotional growth.
- One-fourth of the students wished that schools were more interesting and met more of the students' needs. They felt that school should be a place kids enjoy and should focus less on grades and more on actual learning.
- When asked why they cheated on tests, many students indicated that they lacked confidence or did not know the answers and were afraid of failure or embarrassment. The stress and pressure to pass was another contributing factor.

Many of the responses in the survey raised questions for me. I wondered what it felt like to be aware that schools are in crisis while attending school, being subjected to its requirements, and carrying on with life in general? What is the school experience like for the students who are wise enough to realize (more than half of those surveyed) that they are not being prepared for their life goals?

How can we help students feel ok when they don't understand what they are learning? Are we teaching our children that they should be ashamed if they make a mistake? Making mistakes is actually an important part of discovery. Mistakes can become springboards for great change. Observing the number of students who openly acknowledged stepping away from ethical behavior to fit into the norm raise questions concerning our assessment tools and their authenticity. Students were aware of their motivations for cheating – the need and/or pressure to pass a test or class, along with their lack of confidence or fear of embarrassment. This raises an interesting question: How can schools cultivate confidence in their students, while imbuing a sense that their own personal best is good enough?

Since the stress and pressure to pass overrides many students' codes of ethics, I believe this is an important issue to be considered, in developing schools that support the growth and development of our children. As we saw in the survey results, students are seeking school environments that are student-centered, safe, and less stressful. I can envision policy makers, teachers, students, and administrators striving to develop schools with learning environments where children and young adults are encouraged to reach their potential through self-discovery and authenticity. Can you?

The last question is of even greater importance to me given that two-thirds of the students felt that they received enough personal attention at school. It was disturbing to see that much of these students' needs were rudimentary: needing attractive, safe, non-violent, and clean schools. Experiencing learning that truly challenges their minds, expands their horizons, uncovers their authentic selves, and creates a sense of community was not a viable consideration to these teens. Meeting students and staff's basic needs can only happen if it is deemed important, which is why I am having this discussion.

Contemplative Practices and Inner-City Youth

Between March and April 2009, I offered a meditation class to the after-school program at Schenectady High School. I viewed this as an opportunity to receive feedback from at-risk students who struggle academically. The number of students who attended the program varied daily, ranging from four students to sixteen. Participating students answered survey questions. Responses to the survey are as follows:

SHS After School Program Survey 2009

1. How many times have you attended the relaxation class?
2. Do you find it helpful? How so?
3. Are you more relaxed after coming to the meditation class?
4. Do you find it easier to do your homework after attending the relaxation class?
5. Do you think this class would be beneficial for other students at SHS?
6. Do you think there is a connection between stress management and the relaxation techniques we have practiced in the after-school program?

7. If SHS offered a course in meditation practices, would you be interested in taking it?
8. Which classes did you like the best?
9. Comments:

Results of the survey:

11 students repeated visits to the program on a regular basis
11 students found the program helpful; 4 students did not find the program helpful.

Students who found the class helpful made the following comments: "It makes me feel better; relieves stress"; "It helps me to think bigger; gets things off my chest; calms me down"; It's helps me to relax";" I'm getting peace and quiet"; "It helps me think outside the box"; "It helps me sleep."; "It helps me cope with problems".; It depends on the situation".; "It's necessary for me to slow down".

- 3 students felt they could not calm down even during mediation; 11 students felt more relaxed after the program; 3 did not feel more relaxed.
- 7 students found it easier to do homework afterwards; 2 did not know; 4 did not find it easier to do homework.
- 10 students felt that this program would be helpful to others; 3 did not.
- 12 students felt that there was a connection between stress management and the meditation/relaxation techniques practiced.
- 10 students would take a class in meditation if it were offered during school hours; 3 would not take the class; 1 did not know.

Some really interesting discussions came up in the group, and there were some beautiful, lasting results. The first day we met, there were seven of us in total. I lowered the light and turned on the multimedia television so we could have soft music in the background while I guided the group into deep breathing, relaxation, and silence. We stayed in silence for 15 minutes or so, and then I asked the students if they had anything they wanted to share. A male student whom I will call Jose (I did not know him personally) asked me if my aura always changed colors from blue to purple. He shared that he could see the energy field surrounding my body. (I have sensed the same colors surrounding my body and been told the same thing by healers). Others shared what colors they "saw" or felt. Another student described how she can feel it when others are ill. We allowed all experiences to be accepted, without judgment. It was intimate and lovely, being so comfortable sharing with no prior meeting or agenda. We were all simply being who we are. All six students commented on how relaxed and clear-minded they felt. When I saw two of the students in the hallway the following day, they greeted me with big smiles. One even gave me a hug!

As the weeks progressed, there was a core group of students who consistently returned to each class. A freshman with severe attention challenges told me how much the meditation class was helping him with anger management. Three weeks later, he told me he had been meditating at home, and found it helped him not get car sick when he meditated in the car. The program created an opportunity for me to integrate some of the practices we used in my classes, and I even had the opportunity to offer meditation to students instead of elective study hall during the school day. (Yes, in the middle of the building filed with over 4000 people actively engaging)! This was really exciting because students and staff had the opportunity to experience the cumulative benefits of focused relaxation during the day at school, when they needed it the most.

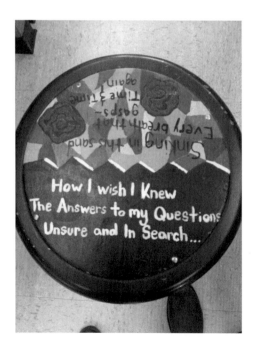

19 Stool from Tom Sarnaki's Class Schenectady High School Student Artist Unknown

Remembering the Magic with International Women's Writing Guild

In June of 2008, I had the wonderful opportunity to chaperone four high school students at the week-long conference hosted by The International Women's Writing Guild (IWWG), *"Remember the Magic,"* held at Skidmore College in Saratoga Springs, NY, 35 minutes from Schenectady. It was the first time that any of the students had been to Saratoga, or to a writing conference – and it was also a first for the guild to host high school students -- so I was excited about this venture! Apart from the four Schenectady High School students, the participants were adult women from several states, Europe, Canada, Mexico, and Southeast Asia. Over 70 workshops were offered during the conference, and the students immersed themselves in various writing workshops whose focus was personal growth and transformation. It did not take long for the students to break off into workshops of their choice, rather than staying together as a group.

During the conference, we had the opportunity to share meals together, discussing our experiences of the various workshops. Driving the students home became an opportunity to further these discussions with transparency and authenticity. The students truly enjoyed sharing their experiences with the women in their workshops, and they very much felt part of the group. They especially enjoyed the opportunity to write from their hearts, without experiencing the typical judgments that occur in an English classroom.

I was amazed at the depth and clarity in which they wrote. Three of the four girls asked to be invited back to the conference and wished that school could be run in workshop-style, offering students the opportunity to explore their creativity through writing with more freedom and support, rather than learning English for a state exam at the end of the year.

In addition to writing workshops, IWWG offered several workshops to enhance creativity and connection to rejuvenate and inspire its attendees.

Through IWWG, I had the rare opportunity to connect with my students on a deep level, because we had the time and space explore writing in an environment that supported my student's creativity. Katarina, Amanda, Fatima, Miad, and Shana benefited from this experience in unexpected ways. How delightful it was to experience growth through the written word, as they shared with heart-felt authenticity!

Sound Healing Workshop at IWWG Skidmore

During one late afternoon session, Katarina and I attended a toning workshop. After introductions, the group was asked to lie on the floor, face up with heads in the center, forming a large circle. Our shoulders were close to one another as we began toning. The group toned for 20 minutes or so and shared our experiences with one another following the exercise. Toning was not new to me and played a key role in my doctoral research. This, however, was not the case for Katarina. Not only was the toning a new experience but lying on the floor in a college chapel with a bunch of old ladies was something she had not anticipated! I checked in with her after the experience and her response was thoughtful and deep. Katarina explained that at first, she thought that the exercise was really weird, and she had to keep herself from giggling, but after about five minutes of toning, she experienced something that changed her perspective profoundly. Katarina began listening to all the sounds, and as her listening grew deeper, she felt as though all the sounds merged into one. She experienced this in her body too. Katarina shared that she "had never felt this relaxed or peaceful before." Her next statement came as a surprise because it was something I have felt for a long time but had not shared with my colleagues or students. Katarina described how relaxed and as ease she felt after doing the exercises that seemed weird to her at first, sharing "We should be doing this in gym," Katarina said. "If students had the opportunity to practice toning, there wouldn't be so many fights in school," she further explained. Katarina's willingness to move beyond her comfort zone is a skill that many students would indeed benefit from. Toning enriched her experience of IWWG, and more importantly, she was able to translate her learning experience into an idea that is relevant to her life, her relationship to herself and to the group.

Thank you so much!. I have never been to a place where there was so much sisterhood. I have never been around so many women who supported each other and were so kind. Things like that, you just don't experience everyday and I may have never experienced that ever in my life if it wasn't for you Hannelore. I appreciate you giving me that experience. Thank you for creating a sanctuary for all women th are independent and aspiring independent young women like myself to gather. I definetly felt the love. - hatarina Lassiter

Dear Ms/Mrs. Hahn
I thank you very much for the opportunity to meet published by most authors. I was very inspired Hilda Ward. of the writers, especially She showed me alot of love and support I thank you alot for allowing me to h lunch with writers. I appreciate it. really could love to be a writer published author. I c be

Dear Hannelore
I would like to thank you for allowing me to experience remembering the magic at Skidmore College. I enjoyed Choosing a class I was interested in, so I can learn. The cafeteria food was fan-tastic. How the campus is situated made me feel like I was in another world with nature. Lots of love.

– Amanda E. Aguas

20 Miad, Fatima & me at International Woman's Writers Guild (Fatima and Miad also stood before the board of education in Literacy of the Heart)

Omega Teen Camp

Omega's experiential classes are inclusive and varied. The teens I met loved the program. One young man from Hollywood, California said, "This is my favorite place in the world. It's a place where I can just be me." Students come from many walks of life. Their schooling ranged from public school to private school and home-schooling experiences. Classes offered on the day I attended camp included pottery, a high ropes course, swimming, world dance, hip hop, relationship skills, meditation, outdoor survival techniques, and reflexology.

I had the privilege to facilitate two one-hour sessions with twenty-four students and three counselors. The short narrative describes my extraordinary encounter with nature at Omega.

I visited Omega Teen Camp the summer of 2008 as a visiting teacher. Omega Institute is one of the largest holistic learning centers in the country and offers opportunities for young adults and adults to explore learning through experience. My niece attended Omega for three years and loved it! It was actually Alex who suggested that I teach there – she thought that I would love the experience, and she was right!

I got to the camp early to get a feel for how things ran there, and to have an opportunity to connect in and relate with the students I'd be working with later in the day. The best way to do this, I decided was by participating in an activity. I headed to the dining hall to see what the students recommended I try. A sweet girl suggested I try the ropes course. I thought I'd give it a try. so off I headed to the ropes course group. It was a beginner class, which was perfect for me. The general idea behind the ropes course, which was to build trust and work as a team was explained to the group by the facilitator, who was a college student, and graduate of the teen camp ropes course.

We gathered in front of a tree, which had a six-foot ladder attached to its trunk, with a small platform above it. The first exercise involved to climbing the latter and standing on the platform facing the tree's trunk. Next, we were instructed to cross our arms over our chest and drop into the awaiting arms of twelve young people who were stationed in two rows with interlocked arms, below. While I waited for my turn, I noticed a hawk above flying in circles. The third circle it made called my attention, and I took a deep breath to listen to what its message might be.

The exercise looked easy enough, I thought to myself – until I stepped on to the platform and realized how high off the ground I actually was. Once again, I spotted the hawk from the corner of my eye and asked for its assistance. I immediately felt its wings surrounding me, and knew that I was ready to trust, and allow myself to fall gracefully backwards into the arms of the group of teens expecting me. I literally felt a set of wings hold me as a dropped into the arms of the cheering group of teens.

After lunch I met with the students I was facilitating. The session was planned to an experiential exploration where the participants had the opportunity to access their inner healer through awareness of their body as energy. Both classes were beautiful experiences, and several students commented on their interest in learning more. Their level of connection with one another's essence as energy was quite amazing. Hugs, giggles, tears of deep knowing and appreciation for being seen as their authentic self, questions and lively, thought-provoking comments arose, extending both sessions beyond the allotted time. I even had three teens ask if I was coming back! Students commented on their innate connection to nature, and how balanced and relaxed they felt after the exercises. They were curious about developing more emotional stability and learning about how emotional stability relates to their body as energy. Several students described their own experiences in working with energy and self-awareness, their sensitivity to other's energy and emotions, and challenges they had in setting boundaries.

I asked each member of the group to choose a partner they didn't know for the exercises. The personal connection and immediate intimacy among partners after the exercise was palpable. Five students mentioned that they had studied Reiki or had other healing modalities at home. The students expressed joy in meeting others who had similar interests and levels of awareness. Several students mentioned that they felt somewhat isolated at home, not being able to share with close friends at the level of depth they experienced as a group setting a clear intention to show up authentically as who they were.

I was touched with the level of openness and gratitude that the students and counselors expressed. I have to wonder how many students in schools across the nation would benefit from experiencing other ways of knowing and being, in a learning environment that supports this process.

Chapter Ten

"A small group of thoughtful (& caring) people could change the world.
Margaret Meade

Integrative Public Education: A New Model Worth Exploring... because we can!!

In this brief, but important chapter, I'd like to share some ideas that might be useful in supporting a paradigm shift in the educational system that would benefit each child's growth and development; intellectually, emotionally, socially, and creatively. It was inspired by my participation at three conferences: 1) The Eighth Scientific Conference in Brain Research in Mindfulness-Based Stress Reduction (MBSR) through the University of Massachusetts, 2) The Third Biennial Interdisciplinary Conference in Brain Development and Learning through the University of British Columbia in Vancouver 3) The Third Healing Sound Symposium at Omega Institute. and the meeting of Indigenous grandmothers at Omega in Rhinebeck, NY.

Integrative Education is based on the idea of developing an open-systemic approach that is fluid, adaptable and resilient, supporting sustainable change and growth. All three conferences model a grass-roots approach to systems change. Let's take a moment to explore how schools can be designed to guide students in reaching their human potential. Imagine what inclusion can look like in a system designed to support learning that is integrated and sustained through life!

In this model:

- **All participating members have the opportunity to experience learning as a lifelong process that is mutually inclusive and supportive.**

- This model's foundation is based on a willingness and commitment to relate to others with an open mind and open heart. It requires nothing less than an earnest effort to courageously explore the personal obstacles and biases we each carry that might inhibit the clarity and quality of our relatedness, and our willingness to move beyond our fears in striving to reach our potential.
- An inclusive "think tank" consisting of individuals who are recognized as "servant leaders" in the field of mindfulness, consciousness, and the practice of non-violent communication with policy makers, legislators, scholars, researchers, administrators, educators, students, and parents can explore the role of education and how it can evolve to meet the needs of our youth today, and in generations to come. The intention for the MBSR (or similar research-based training) is to develop a culture of relating through policy making that continues to grow reflectively, objectively, inclusively, and creatively.
- Ethics are of utmost importance, tempered with a sense of humility in each stakeholder to stay true to our cause of being "child centered" in our approaches.
- Servant Leaders take on the role of "servant leaders" supporting the good of the whole, while allowing for flexibility and autonomy with the needs of individual learning communities (which may or may not take shape in the form of school districts, depending on the assessed needs of the community).
- Servant Leaders would receive direct input from the districts that they serve to develop sustainable growth in the learning community through web casts with intermittent visits to the school community. Relationships fostered by policy makers show they have the best interest in the public (including the children that they serve).
- Policy makers can encourage educational institutions to bridge the gaps in programs that offer contemplative practices and social and emotional learning like mindfulness, sound, rhythm and music and art therapies. It is important to increase dialogue between social scientists and medical researchers to further investigate the relationship between science and daily application of its findings in society.
- School communities would be supported through an integrated model consisting of Universities and Colleges that work directly with the school districts in their vicinity. Grad students could participate in research projects that encourage growth and learning for youth in the areas that are targeted as being critical (including interpersonal skills, like self-awareness and creativity).

- School Communities would be directly linked with community-health centers serving as educational, preventative and intervention programs as needed. Positive dialogue between members is really important for this to work well. This means training must be available for all staff.
- Learning Standards would be used as a measure **in service** to the individual child's growth and development, not to be confused with being used as a competitive, tool that might thwart their own development through the expectation of "being like someone else" or "doing as well as someone else. (This is a non-competitive model of learning)
- Ongoing curriculum development supporting personal growth, self- reflection and stress reduction can be added to core curriculum at all ages.
- Ongoing curriculum development supporting sustainable communities, global awareness and environmental issues including health and well-being of all inhabitants of the planet can be added to core curriculum.
- Local businesses, Non-for Profits and large corporations could receive tax breaks for working with schools in developing "apprentices and school to work programs" that see youth as an investment in our future from a progressive viewpoint that supports human growth, potential and evolution rather than a capitalistic monetary or resource value.
- All stakeholders in this systems approach would be viewed, as equals in the importance of their roles and compensation for their service would be treated as such. All participants can be treated with dignity and respect, because our leadership deeply understands the important role each group plays in creating a system that is indeed systemic and wholesome.

Examples of inclusion at the building level could look something like the following:

- All adults working at the building level are in direct contact with students can model being "lifelong learners". They would be given opportunities to cultivate self-reflective skills and to advance professionally while they are employed with the school district. In this way, students are learning alongside adults who are of the similar socioeconomic and cultural backgrounds aspire to be first-generation college attendees have role models they can relate to and have easy access to. The entire learning community supports "lifelong learning".
- Easy grants (federally or independently funded) made available to teaching staff and teaching assistants to travel and train in areas of their interest and expertise that support sustainability,

inclusion, and lifelong learning) and bring their direct experiences back to the classroom. (Creating connections outside their school district, and develop programs where students engage with people from other regions of the world). Their role is to facilitate learning and bring it to life. This requires being inspired to model life-long learning.

- Paraprofessionals could receive credit towards teacher training programs to increase their knowledge base and grow professionally to compensate for their low paying salaries.

- Custodial staff, paraprofessionals, secretarial staff lunch assistants and could be given opportunities for further training in a related area that they are interested in, and attend the program thought the college that is working directly with the school through adult education programs made available at reduced tuition.

- Time would be set aside to share wheat all participants are learning in an informal setting that is organized by participants from each group of learners.

- Flex schedules support the individual learning communities.

- Flex classes could participate in an exchange programs and collaborative community service programs with schools in neighboring communities of differing socioeconomic backgrounds and ethnicities, funded by businesses to raise awareness. In a model as such, everyone has the opportunity to see their own growth and the value of learning individually and collectively.

- Students would be directly involved in the planning and implementation of lessons that emerge through contemplative exploration of content areas. Ideas like exploring our passions, interests, skills, creativity and sustainability, can become commonplace as school cultures become more self-reflective and responsive.

- Teachers, assistants, counselors, and administrators would be trained in inclusive models that facilitate experiential learning (more like workshops). Self-reflective skills could be cultivated through programs like U Mass's MBSR and NYC's Inner Resilience Program, directed by Linda Lantieri to strengthen their skills and develop increasingly more responsive ways of dealing with the stress that is an unavoidable yet directly part of human connection and life. Both Programs are research-based, with the intent to sustain scientific research in the field. Programs could be tailored to current teaching staff, teachers in training and professors training future teachers.

- Buildings would have a designated place specifically designed to offer "downtime" or quiet time for students and staff during to use to decompress during the day. It would have natural light, plant life and furnishings that reflect its intent, and staff that supervise its use.

- International wi-fi exchange programs can be part of all history classes so students become more socially responsible and globally aware. (teacher training is necessary for this to be affective)
- Schools would be designed as eco-friendly environments that introduce programs to students and staff supporting healthy lifestyles including the use of local agriculture, and food services that support healthy brain development.
- Collaborating community health centers and educational centers could offer continuing training for underserved parents and children in health care issues.
- Human beings, seen as open systems with universal commonalities would reflect openness in relationship to exploring human potential. This is a long-range plan that requires attention to detail while maintaining flexibility.
- Students would have lots of opportunities to experience organized learning activities outside their school community before they graduate. (This would require a powerful infrastructure where accurate assessment for student's needs, and including parents, guardians, and family members)

It is my sincere hope that the synergistic dreams of our future generation will bring more to the table than is imaginable at this point in time.

Chapter Eleven

"Education is what remains after one has forgotten everything he learned in school."
Albert Einstein

Consciousness, Self- Awareness, and Lifelong Learning

Now I understand that like many of my students, I am a highly intuitive, kinesthetic, and auditory learner with an aptitude for writing, singing, and storytelling. I am particularly skilled at exploring and noticing the connections between ideas, experiences, people, and places. These skills were not considered "strengths" in a traditional school setting.

I am curious to hear from young people about their views on learning. I truly believe that they have a wealth of ideas to share on how all schools could become exciting, challenging, life- supporting, and self-sustaining learning environments, expanding, growing, and evolution itself. I love the idea of connecting with young people through the mediums that they're most comfortable working in, even if it means pushing myself to face my own technological phobias!

I wrote Dreaming New Schools in hopes of encouraging discussions about life-long learning that support transformation and growth for all students. In my observation, many teens are compelled to express themselves freely, creating challenges for instructors attempting to work under an authoritative teaching paradigm. Students are searching for experiences that will help them meet the challenges that life offers. Curricula that encourage students to discover their passions, listen to their bodies, explore the non-physical aspects of themselves, and acknowledge their multiple intelligences can be easily enriched through the arts. Sound, rhythm, and music, much like other art forms, can be used to enhance learning, and help students and staff maintain focus, and balance, and include the body in the learning process.

As educators experiment with various mediums, we discover creative ways to engage students learning. Integrating experiential learning activities and using sound, rhythm, and music requires some risk taking, but I hope the chapters on music, sound and healing are useful resources.

Teaching students to acknowledge, honor and respect their body, mind, and creative spirit can help them to recognize that they are an intrinsic part of the learning community. Rosanne Ranari described this experience in her music and drama classes noting, "When the students hear one another … they do shine." Interweaving art-based content areas such as emotional intelligence, human relations, and body-mind awareness into an interdisciplinary program can support this process. I'd love to see programs that support emotional intelligence flourish.

I experienced sound being used as a conscious path to a more enlightened mind in my studies. I have seen sound, rhythm, and music used as vehicles to raise funds for AIDS; to support the women's shelter in Schenectady and the Indigenous Tuva of Mongolia; to give medical support to a Guyanese child and to support schools in South America and Africa. I have seen babies, children, teens, and adults enchanted by the life force that music brings by creating community and healing wounds of the past. Each musical encounter I participated in helped me see the world as a brighter place. I witnessed individuals building bridges, which transcended race and culture, age, and time, by embracing one another in song. I discovered that the harmonic structure created through sound, music, and rhythm has the capacity to cut through the very core of our souls and open our hearts when we least expect it.

I also had the opportunity to explore modalities that I feel passionately about, including multicultural devotional practices using sound, creative artistic expression, holistic education, and transformative learning experiences.

Producing, writing, and editing Dreaming New Schools included experimentation with a broad spectrum of modalities using sound, rhythm, and music from different cultures, encounters, which contributed to my sense of empowerment and self-assuredness. Recognizing that I was an artist played a major role in my personal transformation. Complete immersion in the creative process allowed me the freedom to discover and learn without limitations set by standardized forms of instruction. I envision the same for all students.

You can see that musical experiences aren't limited to musicians and professional dancers. In the final two semesters of my program, I consciously practiced Gardner's multiple intelligences, balancing kinesthetic, visual, spatial, natural, intuitive, intra-personal, and interpersonal learning experiences with the cognitive skills needed to do my research. I took a pause to be in nature, or to sing, dance, or drum when working at the computer became fatiguing and my body needed an energy boost. Integrating sound, rhythm, and music into my research enriched my learning experience and helped me to feel more

Drumming, chanting, yoga, meditation, or freestyle movement releases the energy imbalance I encounter when I get overly excited or tense. Their effectiveness can be profound when I breathe consciously and set a clear intention to stabilize before I begin my practice.

Balancing sound, rhythm, and music with extended periods of silence helps me witness my personal growth and transformation.

balanced, centered, and creative. I noticed that I have much more frenzied outlook and state of mind when I forget to slow down and center myself.

Deep listening skills can cultivate self-awareness and mutuality and can be applied to the classroom. As students and staff become more skilled at listening, they can increase their intuitive skills. These intuitive skills offer opportunity to balance student's energy and help them become more present for their studies. "Our classrooms must find a balance between various learning emphases, such as individual learning and group learning, analytic thinking and intuitive thinking, content and process, and learning and assessment" (Miller 1). Combining instruction with breathing exercises and meditative practices enhances students and staff's ability to maintain balance and focus.

Sound, Rhythm, Music, and the Scientific Community

The scientific community continues to advance and integrate its research, making it applicable to the public. The use of sound, rhythm, music, and the interplay of harmonics as a healing modality have been practiced in Eastern and indigenous cultures across the planet for thousands of years. Social scientists, ethno-musicologists, and computer technologists have helped bridge the gap between ancient traditions and Western science. Access to sound-based contemplative practices has influenced the emergence of harmonics in medical science as well (Cooke, Harris). Art therapies, which were once considered recreational, are now being used in hospitals, nursing homes, children's clinics, and assisted living facilities to promote a sense of well-being, reduce stress, and relieve pain.

Establishing Integrity in Teaching from Multicultural Perspectives

Identifying and meeting the needs of individual learning communities continues to be one of the challenges of educational reform in the 21st century (Meir). It is equally important that we determine the appropriate paradigms shifts attainable for individual learning communities. This process will require strong individuals who can hold a vision for an authentic assessment of the current state of affairs and consideration for the students and staff along with the financial, community, and political support.

Teachers are given the opportunity to fully engage in the creative process increasing their skills in practicing creativity, observation, and objectivity. By honoring the individual human potential inherit in each child we pave the way for a more promising future.

This is especially important to remember as our global community becomes increasingly more accessible. Schools are the perfect place to teach cultural sensitivity. As other perspectives are shared, students learn that each culture has its own unique viewpoint and experience. Because music and rhythm touch the emotions, they can be used to consciously heal wounds of the past and build bridges across cultures, creating a greater sense of a global community and global awareness, right there in the classroom.

It is important to develop curriculum where students and staff can directly experience other cultures. Teacher certification representative of the diverse population in which teachers serve will provide visible role models for schools with diverse populations. Artists, musicians, scholars, authors, educators, and students from other nations can share diverse perspectives in learning.

Our educational system has the potential to create a healing story with our indigenous people, who have a wealth of knowledge, wisdom, and cultural exchange to share. The time is ripe for new paradigms in education

Immersion and active participation through experiential learning makes personal transformation possible because it connects the body, mind, emotions, and creative spirit in a visceral, tactile way that is recorded in the body at the cellular level (Lipton). This sensory experience continues to evolve as the individual chooses to acknowledge and release habitual limiting beliefs.

Music can be a wonderful tool for community service projects to support growth, transformation, and inclusion. Exploring music from multi- and cross-cultural perspectives celebrates unity within diversity. Sound, harmonics and rhythm can also be used to augment the individual learning experience, and music can be used to promote inclusion and celebrate the creative genius of each child. Music from other cultures can be presented with cultural sensitivity, providing youth the opportunity to experience its unique quality.

supporting experiential, transformative learning (Feinstein, Houston). We needn't wait for our government officials to create this story. It is, in fact, the story of building bridges and creating trust that we are committed to repeat until dignity and respect are an actualized in society.

The Influence of Intention

Further explorations in metaphysics, transformative learning and holistic educational will catapult our understanding of learning. Gregory Cajete's model of native science "attempts to connect the 'in-scape' -- our human intelligence, a microcosm of the intelligence of the Earth and the universe -- with the heart and mind." Through this holistic lens, "[a]rt and language, through story, song, and symbolic dance, are used simultaneously to explore the relationship to the in-scape and the land" (Cajete 71). Pilot programs and charter schools are likely candidates for these programs.

Shaun McNiff, Ph. D, Provost, and Dean of Endicott college asks the empirical question "Can the perception and creation of beauty bring healing qualities?". William Shakespeare reminds us, that "beauty is in the eye of the beholder." I agree with Oxford University Professor John Hyman when he says, "We can discover what is really beautiful by learning to give reasons for our preferences ... some things in the world are beautiful — probably many more than we imagine" (Hyman website). To me, beauty is found in the discovery of our Divine creative spirit within. And this project has been a constant state of discovery for me!

From Individuals to One Community

Do our individual thoughts and actions impact the whole, like they did in room D19? I believe they do! I learned first-hand that personal accountability, integrity, and honesty can have a positive influence on teacher and student.

Approaching learning with reverence and conscious intent creates the capacity to teach inclusion, rather than segregation, cooperation rather than confrontation, unity within diversity, respect, dignity, and oneness. "Music awakens the body and brings life to the learning process". (Ranari)

On a personal note, I've learned that our body's energy circuitry is profoundly subject to the external stimuli we experience in each moment. How we choose to respond is very important. Mindful awareness of our energy, thoughts and patterns can help us find balance. Experiencing peace of mind can become a personal choice, moment to moment. The urgent push to achieve that drives large institutions like school systems can find its place in balance with respectful inclusion of our physical body's needs. I've learned that this level of inclusion creates emotional wellbeing, which is necessary for learning to take place. I've witnessed far too many teachers, students, and administrators who barely take time to breathe throughout the day because they have bought into the feelings of urgency dominating their existence, resulting in chronic fatigue, stress, and illness. I was one of those teachers! I learned that creating safe places throughout the day to regroup, refocus, and energize is vital to my body's health and wellbeing. As my students and I practiced self-care we became empowered collectively. We each learned to take responsibility for our actions. We also learned that our actions have a sustaining effect on others.

Generational Beliefs and Educational Changes

We each have our unique biology, life story, and personal circumstances that shaped the person they we today. It is interesting however, to look at the group dynamics within our inherited sub-cultures. I was a baby boomer.

Having grandparents who were born overseas led to my own unique experience of what it meant to be an American citizen born in the late fifties. Speaking from my personal experience raised in a large Italian family. Like many immigrant families, we learned to adapt through struggle and became accustomed to struggling as our parents attempted to forge their own way and raise their families. I am amazed at how quickly human adaptation actually can occur.

Migrating from NYC to suburbia was not without its challenges. This was a time unimaginable to teens today. Before the age of technology and the computer era before the time of globalization and global citizenship. This was a time when it was rare for celebrities and common folk to be seen as political activists, or issues such as citizenship, gender and racism to be publicly advocated against. It was a time when ethnocentric behavior was the cultural norm – in fact, it seemed necessary on some level to maintain and preserve a sense of self-identity while entering an entirely new subculture, thousands of miles from home.

Holding an ethnocentric stance today, no longer serves our growth and development. The Millennial generation is aware of this. Students schooled in urban settings live the "cultural mix" every day. It is their norm, and they have benefited from this experience. We have an opportunity to take this experience a giant leap further and take collective action towards wholeness. We are being called to see, to even understand deeply, that the child we see on the television screen from Uganda, for example, is there to teach us about ourselves. We are witnessing friction, violence, and extreme cases of poverty, and injustice as opportunities to bear witness to the inhumanity in ourselves that is seeking to be healed, unified, and made whole. We are being called to face our inner judge, our inner critic, and to make peace within ourselves, to see our lives as microcosms of the world in which we live. As we learn to embody peace, to love the unlovable aspects of ourselves, we can love others. When we genuinely care enough about our fellow man -- the trickle-down effect is inevitable! Future generations have the opportunity to witness the people rise up and take creative ownership for our lives. There are Gandhi's and Dr. King's in our midst! What we choose to pay attention to, will make all the difference in the world. This is so even now. Who will dream our future if we do not?

This inward journey of Body, Mind and Spirit can become an outward journey of self-expression and sovereignty. It is a journey of discovering unity within diversity, acknowledging our unique ways of seeing the world, and expressing ourselves. It requires servant-leaders who are aware of the important role we play as leaders. We become more and more comfortable sharing leadership because we understand that each person contributing is equal. We do not see ourselves as "better" or "less" than those we serve. Humanity serves one another. We seek the good of the whole, and the individual collectively. We listen to one another before reacting. We own our vulnerability and become willing to heal the child within who seeks safety.

In conclusion, I respectfully ask you to take time to consider the following questions:

- What does learning mean to you?
- Is intellectual pursuit the most valid means of knowing, or understanding?
- Can we heal the disconnect of our human spirit from our body and cherished planet?
- How can we, as parents, educators and servant-leaders act and become sacred social activists and help our children reach their own unique potential?

We entrust the lives of our precious offspring to an institution that has the potential to inspire then to become they are meant to be. Our educational system can be evaluated by the standards of the twenty first century, and the global awareness we now have at our fingertips and in our hearts. Together, we can create a reality that is based on love, on creativity, unity, and mutual respect.

It is my hope that this discussions about life-long learning become part of our everyday conversations so we can have a positive, sustaining impact on educating youth. I believe we can make a difference. I also believe it is worthwhile to imagine future educational models where our youth participate equally in the learning process, and their ideas are seen as integral to the programs they engage with. I invite you to join me in this discussion if it seems worthwhile to you as well.

Our deepest fear is not that we are inadequate. Our deepest fear is that we are powerful beyond measure.

It is our light, not our darkness that most frightens us.
We ask ourselves who am I to be brilliant, gorgeous, talented, fabulous?
Actually, who are you not to be? You are a child of God.

Your playing small does not serve the world. There's nothing enlightened about shrinking so that other people won't feel insecure around you.

We are all meant to shine, as children do. We were born to make manifest the glory of God that is within us.

It's not just in some of us; it's in everyone.

And as we let our own light shine, we unconsciously give other people permission to do the same.

As we're liberated from our own fear, our presence automatically liberates others.

- Marianne Williamson

21 Our Greatest fear

May all children be inspired to reach their potential,
Through creative collaboration, clear intention
and loving guidance.

Works Cited

American Heritage Dictionary. http:\American Heritage Dictionary.com

Aposhyan S. *Natural Intelligence* ~ Body Mind Integration and Human Development. BMP: Boulder Colorado, 1997.

Arrien, Angeles. *The Four-fold Way: Walking the Path of The Warrior, Teacher, Healer, And Visionary*. San Francisco: Harper, 1993.

Beaulieu, John. *Music and Sound in the Healing Arts*. New York: Station Hill Press, 1997.

Beaulieu, John. Human Tuning. *Sound Healing with Tuning Forks*. Biosonics Enterprises, Ltd. High Falls, NY., 2010.

Berendt, Joachim - Earnst. *Nada Brahma ~ The World is Sound* Music and the landscape of consciousness. Rochester, VT: Destiny Books, 1983.

Blanc, Darlita. "Being a Decent Human Being is a Modern Way to be a Warrior," UD Dept. of Education Educational Resource Center: Sept 2003.

Blumenfield, Larry. *Voices of Forgotten Worlds*. New York: Roslyn, 1993.

Bohart, A. "Intuition and Creativity." Journal of Constructivist Psychology. 12(2004): 287-311.

Broomfield, John. *Other Ways of Knowing*. Vermont: Inner Traditions, 1997.

Brucia, D. and Cooke-Moffitt, P. "Multicultural Sound Healing." Handout. Sauselito, California. Nov. 10-11, 2001.

Bructsck, Jane. *The Multiple Intelligence Lesson Plan Book*. Healdsburg: University Press, 1995.

Buzan, T and Buzan, B. *The Mind Map Book*. New York: Penguin Books Inc, 1996.

Cajete, Gregory. *Igniting the Spark*. Santa Fe: Clear Light Publishers, 2000.

Catto, Jaime and Bridgeman, Duncan. *One Giant Leap*. DVD. New York: Palm Pictures, 2001.

Chandler, Yosama.http\\: www.Ychallenor@cox.net.

Chopra, Deepak. "How to Know God." Seminar. Omega Institute. Rhinebeck, NY. July 12-16, 2004.

... *The Deeper Wound Recovering the Soul from Fear and Suffering*. New York: Harmony. 2001.

Chopra, Deepak and Goswami, Amit. "The Quantum Physics of Soul and Spirit". Audiotape. New York: Hayhouse.com.

Cooke, Pat Moffitt. "Multicultural Sound Healing." Seminar. Sausalito, Nov. 10-11, 2001.

Deitrich, Arne. "Neurocognitive mechanisms underlying the experience of flow." Consciousness and Cognition. 13(2004):746-761.

Dirkx, JM. "Transformative Learning in Action: Insights from Practice." Nurturing the Soul. Jossey & Bass: San Francisco, 1997. 78-79.

... "Musings and Reflections on the Meaning, Context, and Process of Transformative Learning." Journal of Transformative Learning. 2 April 2006:123-139.

"Dr, Phil". With Philip McGraw. WNBC, New York. 23 August 2004.

Feinstein, David. "The Psychology of Myths." Lecture. Leadership Training in Social Artistry, University of Southern Oregon, Ashland Oregon. June 17, 2004.

Feinstein. "The Psychology of Myths." Pamphlet. Leadership Training in Social Artistry, University of Southern Oregon, Ashland Oregon. June 17, 2004.

Gardner, Howard. *Intelligence Reframed* Multiple Intelligences for the 21st Century. New York: Basic Books, 1999.

Gardner. The Arts and Human Development. New York: Basic Books, 1993.

Goertzel, Ben. "Patterns of Awareness" www.goertzel.org/dynapsyc/panpsychist.htm.

Goertzel, Ben, Germine, Mark, and Combs, Alan. "The Dynamics of Thought, Reality, and Consciousness." http://www.goertzel.org/dynapsyc/2003/intro.htm.

Goldman, Jonathan. *Healing Sound*. Rockport: Element Books, 1992.

Goldman. "Power of Harmonics and Chanting." 8/27/04. www.healingsounds.com.

Grof, Stanislav. The *Holotropic Mind*. Harper: San Francisco, 1990.

Halpern, Steven. *Sound Health*. San Francisco: Harper & Row, 1985.

Harris, Bill. *Thresholds of the Mind*. Beaverton: Centerpointe Press, 2002.

Keys, Laurel E. *Toning*. Marina Del Rey: DeVorss & Co, 1973.

Jourdain, Robert. *Music, the Brain, and Ecstasy*. New York: Harper Collins, 1997.

Lucas, Charles. "Spirit of Complexity." goertzel.org/dynapsyc/1999/spirit.htm.

McCarthy, Sherry. "Teaching Emotional Intelligence." The Delta Kappa Gamma Bulletin. 67 (4):13-16.

McNiff, Shaun. *Art- Based Research*. Philadelphia: Jessica Kingsley Publishers, 1998.

McWhinney, W. and Marcos. "Transformative Education Across the Threshold." Journal of Transformative Learning. 1. 2003:16-37.

Miller, Ron. What are Schools For? Holistic Education in American Culture. Brandon, Vermont: Holistic Education Press, 1997.

Miller. *New Directions in Education*. Brandon, Vermont: Holistic Education Press, 1990.

Mezirow, Jack. "Transformative Learning Theory." New Directions for Adult and Continuing Education. Summer. 1997:5-12.

Morgan, Ponticwlli, Gordon. "Rethinking Creativity". Phi Delta Kappa Fastbacks. 458. (2000): 7-39.

Moustakas, Clark. *Heuristic Research*: Design, Methodology and Applications. Beverly Hills: Sage, 1990.

Myss, Carolyn. *Sacred Contracts*. New York: Three Rivers, 2003.

Petro, Marina. *Angel Ascending*. Online Gallery Dec 15, 2005. www.marinapetro.com

Redmond Layne. *Roots of Awakening*. Chanting the Chakras. CD-ROM New York Interworld 1997.

Rogers, Natalie. *The Creative Connections* Palo Alto: Science & Behavior Books, 1993.

Talbot, Michael. *The Holographic Universe*. New York: Harper Perennial, 1992.

Thompson, Jeffery. "Entrain Your Brain." Center for Neuroacoustic Research. 1/15/04

Weinberger, N.M. "Creating Creativity with Music." Music Research Notes. VI.2 (1998):5.

Zohar, Dana. *The Quantum Self.* New York: Quill, 1990.

Zohar, Danah and Marshall, Ian. *Spiritual Intelligence.* New York: Bloomsbury, 2000.

Zell, Oberon and Babriel, Lisa. "The Millenial Gaia." Pamphlet. Thea Genesis LLC, 1998.

References Consulted But Not Cited

Alfano, Jorge. *Inti ~ mystical Music of the Andes*. Hollywood: Lyrihcord Disks Inc., 1996.

---. *Sacred Sounds*. Audiotape. Hollywood: The Relaxation Company, 1996.

Arguelles Jose. *The Mayan Factor*. Boulder, CO.: Bear & Company, 1987.

---. "The Wisdom Way." Lecture. Leadership Training in Social Artistry, University of Southern Oregon, Ashland Oregon. June 17,1997.

Author, Maia. "Grace Frequency& Energy Experienced as Grace." Class and Interview. Cochiti Lake, New Mexico. July 24, 2002.

Bear, Sun. *Dancing with the Medicine Wheel*. New York: Simon & Schuster, 1991.

---. "Cranial Explorations and Exercises." 8/27/2004. http//biosonics.com

Berg, D. N., and Smith, K. The Self in Social Inquiry. Newbury Park: Sage, 1985.

Biermann, Derek. *Samadhi*. Boston: Shambala, 2000.

Bonny, H. and Savary, L. *Music and Your Mind*. Barrytown: Station Hill Press, 1983.

Camilleri, Vanessa. "Therapist self-awareness: an essential tool in music therapy." The Arts in Psychotherapy. 28.1(Feb 2001): 79-85.

Campbell, Don. *Music for the Mozart Effect*. CD-ROM Laser disc. Boulder: Spring Hill Music, 1997.

---. Music, Physician for Times to Come. Wheaton: Quest, 1990.

Campbell, Joseph and Moyers, Bill. *The Message of the Myth*. Video. New York: Mystic Fire Video, 1988.

---. Masks of Eternity. Video. New York: Mystic Fire Video, 1988.

---. The Hero's Journey. Video. New York: Wellspring Media, 1999.

Carrier, Henry, and Williams Donald. "A Grassroots Approach to Formulating a

Catto, Jaime. "Interview & Video Footage Request." E mail to Jaime Catto. 11/13/04.

Cedillos, Jose. "Second Core Reader Report." E mail to Angela Benedetto. May 25, 2005.

---. E mail. "Second Core Reader Report. E mail to Angela Benedetto. May 25, 2005.

Coffey, A. and Atkinson, P. Making Sense of Qualitative Data. Thousand Oaks: Sage, 1993

Cole, H. and Sarnoff, D. "Creativity and Counseling." Lecture. 25th Annual Creative Problem Solving Conference, Buffalo, NY. June 24, 1979.

Colorio, Elizabeth. "Cymatics Today." 8/27/2004. http://www.cymatics.com

Cooke- Moffitt, P. Shaman, *Jhankri & Nele:* Music Healers of Indigenous Cultures. Text &CD-ROM. Roslyn, NY: Ellipsis Arts, 1997.

Cousineau, Phil. "Myths, Music & Healing: A Conversation with Mike Pinder." Connections: 2 (1997): 36.

Dale-Lopez, Marcia. "Consciousness, the Energy Body and Intuitive Processes." Interview By Angela Benedetto. Schylerville, NY. May 24, 2005.

Diallo, Yaya. "At the Threshold of the African Soul." INTER Culture 141 (2001):1-64.

Emoto, Masuru. *Love Thyself.* Tokyo: Hado Kyoikusha. 2004.

Gagan, Jeanette. *Journeying Where Shamanism and Psychology Meet.* Santa Fe: Rio Chama Publications, 1998.

Gardner, Kay. *Drone Zone healing music.* CD. Roslyn, NY: The Relaxation Co., 1996.

---. Music as Medicine. Audiocassette and text. Boulder: Sounds True, 2000.

Gass, Robert. *Discovering Spirit in Sound.* Audio & Text, NY: Random House, 1999.

Gaynor, Mitchell. *The Healing Power of Sound.* Boston: Shambhala, 2002.

Germine, Mark. "The One Mind Model: Virtual Brain States and Nonlocality of ERP." Http://www.goertzel.org/dynapsyc/2003/onemind.htm.

Grey, Alex. *Sacred Mirrors.* Inner Traditions: Rochester, 1990.

Hagans, Bethe "Art Based Research: Healing Self within the Community of Scholarship." Seminar. TUI&U Vermont College, Montpelier, VT.4/9-13/04.

Hall, James. *Sangoma.* New York: Touchstone, 1994.

Harris, William. Holosync. Introduction CD. Beaverton: Centerpointe Research Institute, 2004.

Hopefisher, Chaula. *Multicolored Chant.* Boston: Chaula Yoga & Music, 1999.

Houston, Jean. *The Mythic Life.* San Francisco: Harper 1996.

Houston, Jean. *Passion For the Impossible.* San Francisco: Harper, 1997.

Houston, Vaas. "Introduction." www.American_Sanskrit_Institute.com 2004.

Hwoschinsky, C. *"Compassionate Listening."* Lecture. Leadership Training in Social Artistry Conference. University of Southern Oregon, Ashland Oregon 9/13/04.

Josephson, Brian. *"String Theory, Universal Mind, and the Paranormal."* Research Notes. Dept. of Physics: University of Cambridge. Sept.2005.

Jung, Carl Gustav. *The Archetypes and the Collective Unconscious.* Translated RFC. Hull. Princeton. Princeton University Press, 1969.

Kaschub, Michelle. "Defining Emotional Intelligence in Music Education." Arts Education Policy Review 103 (2003): 9-15.

Kestrel, Rachel. The Soul of Education Helping Students find Connection, Compassion, and Character at School. Alexander: Association for Supervision and Curriculum Development, 2000.

Kreiger, S. Social Science and the Self: Personal Essays on an Art Form. NJ: Rutgers University Press, 1991.

Kronon, R. "The Basis for Psychoenergetic Phenomena." 5/7/2003. http://www.kronon-offshore. com/Health-en/psychoeneretics.htm.

Lawton, http://www.vanderbilt.edu/AnS/psychology/healthpsychology/TOMATIS.html

Lewiston, David. Trance 1 Sufi Dervish Rite Tibetan Overtone Chant Indian Dhrupad. CD-ROM. New York: Musical Expeditions, 1995.

Linds, Warren. Unfolding Body Mind. Brandon, Vermont: Foundation for Educational Review, 1991.

Lipton, Bruce. The Biology of Belief., Videocassette. Spirit 2000.

Lobell, John. Joseph Campbell, the Man and His Ideas. Joseph Campbell Foundation,1993.

Lorimer, David. *The Third Ear and the Healing Forces of Music*. San Francisco: Element Books, 1988.

Namancura, Juan. "Mapuche Cosmology." Lecture. Sivivana Ashram, Livingston Manor, NY. October 6, 2001.

Newham, Paul. *The Singing Cure*. Audio and Study Guide. Sounds True: Boulder Co, 1998.

Nhat Hanh, Thich. *Living Buddha, Living Christ*. NY: Riverhead Books 1995.

Patton, Michael Quinn. "Two Decades of developments in Qualitative Inquiry." Qualitative Social Work 1. (2002): 261-283. Thousand Oaks: Sage, 2002.

Peterson, Peter. "Cymatics- The Science of the Future. mysticalsun.com.

Petro, Marina. "Consciousness, Intuition and Artmaking" Interview. Saratoga Springs NY May 24, 2005.

Pewewardy, Cornel. "Our Children Can't Wait, Recapturing the Essence of Indigenous Schools in the United States." Cultural Survival Quarterly. 22. (1998): 29-34.

Pinedas, Don Jose. "Curandero Healing Session." New York: July 13, 2002.

Ponce De Leon. *In Search of the Wise One*. Woodside: Bluestar, 1995.

_____. *The Wisdom of the Ancient One*. Woodside: Bluestar, 1995.

Poonswassie, Ann and Charter, Ann. "An Aboriginal Worldview of Helping; Empowering Approaches." Canadian Journal of Counseling 35. (2001): 63-73.

Powell, Richard, Fussell, Linda, Troutman, Porter, Smith, Martha, and Skoog, Gerald. "Toward an Integrative Multicultural Learning Environment." Middle School Journal. 29 (1998):3-13.

Purse, J. Overtone Chanting Meditations. London: Inner Sound, 1992.

Quisenberry, N. and Mcintyre, D. Educators Healing Racism. Association of Teacher Educators and Association for Childhood Education International, 1993.

Ramon, Gallegos Nava. Holistic Education A Pedagogy of Universal Love. Brandon, Vermont: Foundation for Educational Renewal, 2001.

Reason, P. and Rowen, J. Human Inquiry in Action: A Sourcebook of New Paradigm Research. NY: John Wiley & Sons, 1981.

Sands, Jaime. Dancing the Dream. The Seven Sacred Paths of Transformation. Harper Collins Inc.: San Francisco, 1999.

Sanyal, Ritwik. The Lyrical Tradition of Dhrupad 4. CD-ROM. Austria: Makar,1995.

Secakuku, Alph. Songs from the Fourth World Pleasant Music from Hopi Land. DC-ROM. Boulder CO. Red Feather Productions, 1995.

Spadaro, Patricia. "The Metaphysics of Sound." http://www.cymatics.org.

Storr, Anthony. Music and the Mind. Ballantine: New York, 1992.

Ward, Terri, MA. "Small Learning Community Teacher Training." Lecture. Schenectady High School, Schenectady, NY. July 5-10, 2004.

Weinberger, N.M. "Brain Anatomy and Music." Musical Research Notes. VI.2, (1999): 6-7.

---. "What the Brain Tells us about Music: Amazing Facts and Astounding Implications Revealed." Musical Research Notes VII.3 (2000): 8.

Wengrower, Hilda. "Art therapies in educational settings: An intercultural encounter." The Arts in Psychotherapy. 28. 2 (2001) :109-115.

Willis, Pauline. The Reflexology Manual. Rochester: Healing Arts Press, 1996.

Wittimer, Joe. Valuing Similarity and Diversity. Educational Media Corporation: Minneapolis, 1992.

Woldzislaw, Duch. "Physics of Consciousness." IV National Conference on Models of Biological Systems. Nicholas Copernicus University, Torun, Poland.

Wolf, Fred Alan. The Eagle's Quest. New York: Touchstone, 1992.

Wolman, Richard. Thinking with your Soul. NY: Harmony, 2001.

Zinn, Jon-Kabat. Wherever You Go, There You Are. Mindfulness Meditation Practices in Everyday Life. NY: Harmony, 1994.

Index

V

W

Printed in the United States
by Baker & Taylor Publisher Services